THE CONCISE
ERIC CLAPTON

DISTRIBUTED BY

HAL•LEONARD™
CORPORATION
WINONA, MN 55987 MILWAUKEE, WI 53213

THE CONCISE
ERIC CLAPTON

WISE PUBLICATIONS
LONDON/NEW YORK/PARIS/SYDNEY/COPENHAGEN/MADRID

EXCLUSIVE DISTRIBUTORS:
MUSIC SALES LIMITED
8/9 FRITH STREET,
LONDON W1V 5TZ, ENGLAND.
MUSIC SALES PTY LIMITED
120 ROTHSCHILD AVENUE,
ROSEBERY, NSW 2018,
AUSTRALIA.

ORDER NO. AM91921
ISBN 0-7119-4037-1

COMPILED BY PETER EVANS
BOOK DESIGN BY STUDIO TWENTY, LONDON
COVER PHOTOGRAPH BY TERRY O'NEILL

PRINTED IN THE UNITED KINGDOM BY
PAGE BROS, NORWICH.

IN BOTH 'THE LYRICS' AND 'THE MUSIC' SECTIONS
EACH SONG BEARS THE SAME NUMBER, AS LISTED BELOW...

AFTER MIDNIGHT 3
ALBERTA 1
ANYTHING FOR YOUR LOVE 2
BAD LOVE 5
BADGE 4
BEFORE YOU ACCUSE ME 6
BELL BOTTOM BLUES 7
BETTER MAKE IT THROUGH TODAY 8
BLUES POWER 9
CAN'T FIND MY WAY HOME 10
COCAINE 11
COMIN' HOME 13
CROSSROADS 12
GET READY 14
GIVE ME STRENGTH 15
HAVE YOU EVER LOVED A WOMAN 16
HELLO OLD FRIEND 17
HOODOO MAN 18
I CAN'T HOLD OUT 19
I CAN'T STAND IT 20
I FEEL FREE 21
IF I DON'T BE THERE BY MORNING 22
KEY TO THE HIGHWAY 23
KNOCKIN' ON HEAVEN'S DOOR 24
LAWDY MAMA 25
LAY DOWN SALLY 26
LAYLA 27
LEAD ME ON 29
LET IT GROW 30
LONELY STRANGER 28
MAINLINE FLORIDA 31
MEAN OLD FRISCO 32
MOTHERLESS CHILDREN 33
NO ALIBIS 35
NOBODY KNOWS YOU WHEN YOU'RE DOWN AND OUT 36
OLD LOVE 37
ONE MORE CHANCE 38
PLEASE BE WITH ME 34
PRESENCE OF THE LORD 39
PRETENDING 40
RAMBLIN' ON MY MIND 42
ROLL IT OVER 41
ROLLIN' AND TUMBLIN' 43
RUNNING ON FAITH 44
SPOONFUL 46
STEADY ROLLIN' MAN 47
STRANGE BREW 48
SUNSHINE OF YOUR LOVE 49
TALES OF BRAVE ULYSSES 45
TEARS IN HEAVEN 50
TELL THE TRUTH 51
THE SHAPE YOU'RE IN 53
TOO BAD 52
WATCH YOURSELF 54
WHITE ROOM 55
WHY DOES LOVE GOT TO BE SO SAD? 56
WONDERFUL TONIGHT 57
WORRIED LIFE BLUES 58

THE LYRICS

1

ALBERTA

Alberta, Alberta, where ya been so long?
Alberta, Alberta, where ya been so long?
Ain't had no lovin' since you been gone.

Alberta, Alberta, where'd you stay last night?
Alberta, Alberta, where'd you stay last night?
Come home this mornin', clothes don't fit you right.

Alberta, Alberta, girl you're on my mind.
Alberta, Alberta, girl you're on my mind.
Ain't had no lovin' in such a great, long time.

Alberta, Alberta, where you been so long?
Alberta, Alberta, where you been so long?
Ain't had no lovin' since you've been gone.

WORDS & MUSIC BY HUDDIE LEDBETTER.

2

ANYTHING FOR YOUR LOVE

God's got a plan, He's making it clear,
Sweet little love song in your ear,
Like heads made of diamond, love will prevail,
Put a little wind in your sail.

And I'd do anything, anything you can dream of,
I'd do anything, anything for your love,
For your love.

Listen now baby, I'm gonna tell you true,
Just how much that I love you,
Got a sweet feeling, I know is real,
This kind of love you can't conceal.

And I'd do anything, anything you can dream of,
I'd do anything, anything for your love,
For your love.
I'd do anything, anything you can dream of,
I'd do anything, anything for your love,
For your love, for your love, for your love,
for your love ...

WORDS & MUSIC BY JERRY LYNN WILLIAMS.

3
AFTER MIDNIGHT

After midnight, we gonna let it all hang down,
After midnight, we're gonna chugalug and shout.
Gonna stimulate some action,
We're gonna get some satisfaction,
We're gonna find out what it is all about.
After midnight, we gonna let it all hang down.

After midnight, we're gonna shake your tambourine,
After midnight, 's all gon' be peaches and cream.
Gonna cause talk and suspicion,
We're gonna give an exhibition,
We're gonna find out what it is all about.
After midnight, we gonna let it all hang down.

WORDS & MUSIC BY J.J. CALE.

4
BADGE

Thinkin' 'bout the times you drove in my car.
Thinkin' that I might have drove you too far.
And I'm thinkin' 'bout the love that you laid on
my table.
I told you not to wander 'round in the dark.
I told you 'bout the swans, that they live in the park.
Then I told you 'bout our kid, now he's married
to Mabel.

Yes, I told you that the light goes up and down.
Don't you notice how the wheel goes 'round.
And you better pick yourself up from the ground
Before they bring the curtain down.
Yes before they bring the curtain down.
Talkin' 'bout a girl that looks quite like you.
She didn't have the time to wait in the queue.
She cried away her life since she fell off the cradle.

WORDS & MUSIC BY ERIC CLAPTON & GEORGE HARRISON.

5

BAD LOVE

Oh what a feeling I get when I'm with you,
You take my heart into everything you do.
And it makes me sad for the lonely people,
I walked that road for so long.
Now I know that I'm one of the lucky people,
Your love is making me strong.

Had enough bad love,
I need something I can be proud of.
Had enough bad love, no more bad love.

And now I see that my life has been so blue,
With all the heartaches I had till I met you.
But I'm glad to say now that's all behind me,
With you here by my side.
And there's no more memories to remind me,
Your love will keep me alive.

Had enough bad love,
I need something I can be proud of.
Had enough bad love, no more bad love.

Had enough bad love,
I need something I can be proud of.
Had enough bad love, no more bad love.

WORDS & MUSIC BY ERIC CLAPTON & MICK JONES.

6

BEFORE YOU ACCUSE ME

Before you accuse me, take a look at yourself.
Before you 'cuse me, take a look at yourself.
You say I'm spendin' my money on other women,
You takin' money from someone else.

I called your mama 'bout three or four nights ago.
I called your mama 'bout three or four nights ago.
Well, your mama said "Son don't call my daughter
no more."

Before you 'cuse me, take a look at yourself.
Before you 'cuse me take a look at yourself.
You say I'm spendin' my money on other women,
You takin' money from someone else.

Come on back home, baby, try my love
one more time.
Come on back home, baby, try my love
one more time.
You know if things don't go to suit you,
I think I'll lose my mind.

Before you 'cuse me, take a look at yourself.
Before you 'cuse me, take a look at yourself.
You say I'm spendin' my money on other women,
You takin' money from someone else.

WORDS & MUSIC BY EUGENE MCDANIELS.

7

BELL BOTTOM BLUES

Bell bottom blues you made me cry,
I don't wanna lose this feeling.
If I could choose a place to die
It would be in your arms.

Do you wanna see me crawl across the floor to you?
Do you wanna hear me beg you to take me back?
I'd gladly do it because I don't want to fade away,
Give me one more day, please, I don't want to
fade away,
In your heart I want to stay.

It's all wrong, but it's all right,
The way that you treat me, baby.
Once I was strong but I lost the fight
You won't find a better loser.
Do you wanna see me crawl across the floor to you?
Do you wanna hear me beg you to take me back?
I'd gladly do it because I don't want to fade away,
Give me one more day, please, I don't want to
fade away,
In your heart I want to stay.

Bell bottom blues don't say goodbye,
We're surely gonna meet again,
And if we do don't you be surprised
You could find me with another lover.

Do you wanna see me crawl across the floor to you?
Do you wanna hear me beg you to take me back?
I'd gladly do it because I don't want to fade away,
Give me one more day, please, I don't want to
fade away,
In your heart I want to stay.

I don't want to fade away, give me one more day,
please,
I don't want to fade away, in your heart I want to stay.
In your heart I want to stay.

WORDS & MUSIC BY ERIC CLAPTON.

8

BETTER MAKE IT THROUGH TODAY

"Life is what you make it,"
That's what the people say,
And if I can't make it through tomorrow
I better make it through today.

I have had my share of troubles,
It's nothing new to me,
When I look around me
All I see is misery.

"Life is what you make it."
At least that's what the people say,
And if we can't make it through tomorrow
We better make it through today.
Through today. Through today.

WORDS & MUSIC BY ERIC CLAPTON.

9
BLUES POWER

Bet you didn't think I knew how to rock and roll.
Oh, I've got the boogie woogie right down in my
very soul.
There ain't no need for me to be a wallflower,
'Cause now I'm livin' on blues power.

I knew all the time, but now I'm gonna let you know:
I'm gonna keep on rockin', no matter if it's fast
or slow.
Ain't gonna stop until the twenty-fifth hour,
'Cause now I'm livin' on blues power.

Well I bet you didn't think I knew how to
rock and roll.
Oh, I've got the boogie woogie right down in my
very soul.
There ain't no need for me to be a wallflower,
'Cause now I'm livin' on blues power.

10
CAN'T FIND MY WAY HOME

Come down off your throne and leave your body alone;
Somebody must change.
You are the reason I've been waiting so long;
Somebody holds the key.

Well I'm weary and I just ain't got the time,
And I'm wasted and I can't find my way home.

Come down on your own and leave your body alone;
Somebody must change.
You are the reason I've been waiting all these years;
Somebody holds the key.

Well I'm weary and I just ain't got the time,
And I'm wasted and I can't find my way home.

Oooh, but I can't find my way home.
Oooh, but I can't find my way home.
Oooh, but I can't find my way home.
Oooh, but I can't find my way home.
Oooh, but I can't find my way home.

11
COCAINE

If you wanna hang out, you've gotta take her out,
cocaine.
If you wanna get down, down on the ground, cocaine.
She don't lie, she don't lie, she don't lie, cocaine.

If you got bad news, you wanna kick them blues,
cocaine.
When your day is done, and ya wanna run, cocaine.
She don't lie, she don't lie, she don't lie, cocaine.

If your thing is gone, and ya wanna ride on, cocaine.
Don't forget this fact, can't get back, cocaine.
She don't lie, she don't lie, she don't lie, cocaine.
She don't lie, she don't lie, she don't lie, cocaine.

12
CROSSROADS

I went down to the crossroad, fell down on my knees.
Down to the crossroad, fell down on my knees.
Asked the Lord above for mercy;
Take me, if you please.

I went down to the crossroad, tried to flag a ride.
Down to the crossroad, tried to flag a ride.
Nobody seemed to know me,
Everybody passed me by.

Well, I'm goin' down to Rosedale, take my rider by
my side.
Goin' down to Rosedale, take my rider by my side.
We can still barrel house baby,
On the river side.

You can run, you can run; tell my friend
Boy Willie Brown.
Run, you can run; tell my friend, Boy Willie Brown
That I'm standin' at the crossroad.
Believe I'm sinkin' down.

13
COMIN' HOME

Been out on the road 'bout six months too long.
I want you so bad, I can hardly stand it.
I'm so tired and I'm all alone.
We'll soon be together, and that's it,
I'm comin' home to your love.

Hitch hikin' on the turnpike all day long.
Nobody seemed to notice just pass me over.
To keep from goin' crazy, I gotta sing my song.
Got a whole lot of lovin' and baby that's why
I'm comin' home to your love.

14
GET READY

Ready, get ready, ready, he's a man who's gonna break
your heart.
Ready, get ready, ready, he's a man who's gonna break
your heart.

You've been foolin' 'round and I don't know why,
Leave me on my own, sittin' high and dry.
But I'm gonna get you back, just you wait and see,
You can't do those things that you're doin' to me.

Ready, get ready, ready, he's a man who's gonna break
your heart.
Ready, get ready, ready, he's a man who's gonna break
your heart.

I've never needed a runnin' 'round dizzy hound
Checkin' out the bitches in heat,
You've got a lotta nerve, dishing out what you serve,
Wagglin' your piece of meat.

Ready, get ready, ready, he's a man who's gonna break
your heart.
Ready, get ready, ready, he's a man who's gonna break
your heart.

I wanna get revenge on your sinful sins,
I gotta get you back for what you did back then.
And now you've got it back life is misery,
Part of you is a part of me.

Ready, get ready, ready, he's a man who's gonna break
your heart.
Ready, get ready, ready, he's a man who's gonna break
your heart.

I wanna get revenge on your sinful sins,
I gotta get you back for what you did back then.
And now you've got it back life is misery,
Part of you is a part of me.

15
GIVE ME STRENGTH

Dear Lord, give me strength to carry on.
Dear Lord, give me strength to carry on.
My home may be out on the highway,
Lord, I've done so much wrong,
So please, give me strength to carry on.

Dear Lord, give me strength to carry on.
Dear Lord, give me strength to carry on.
My home may be out on the highway,
Lord, I've done so much wrong,
But Lord, give me strength to carry on.

WORDS & MUSIC BY ERIC CLAPTON.

16
HAVE YOU EVER LOVED A WOMAN

Have you ever loved a woman
So much you really hate to be alone?
Have you ever loved a woman
So much you really hate to be alone?
When all the time you know
That little girl, li'l' girl, well, done you wrong.

What it does to love a woman
So much it really makes you tremble in pain.
When you love a woman,
So much it really makes you tremble in a pain.
And the part that hurts you bad,
When you never, well, you never gonna see her again.

Have you ever loved a woman
So much it really, really hurts to be alone?
Have you ever loved a woman
So much you really, really hate to be alone?
All the time you know she'll naturally break up your happy home.

WORDS & MUSIC BY BILLY MYLES.

17
HELLO OLD FRIEND

As I was strolling down the garden path,
I saw a flower glowing in the dark.
It looked so pretty and it was unique;
I had to bend down just to have a peek.

Hello old friend, it's really good to see you once again.
Hello old friend, it's really good to see you once again.

I saw you walking underneath the stars;
I couldn't stop 'cause I was in a car.
I'm sure the distance wouldn't be too far;
I got out and walked to where you are.

Hello old friend, it's really good to see you once again.
Hello old friend, it's really good to see you once again.

An old man passed me on the street today;
I thought I knew him, but I couldn't say.
I stopped to think if I could place his frame,
But when he tipped his hat I knew his name.

Hello old friend, it's really good to see you once again.
Hello old friend, it's really good to see you once again.

18
HOODOO MAN

Well I wonder what's exactly the matter,
Child d'you know the time, seemed like an hour.
Ev'rything had changed,
But I hold up my head,
Well I'm just tryin' to make you understand.
Well now ev'rybody tells me.
Somebody HooDoo the HooDoo man.

Well now I buzzed your bell this morning,
You had your elevator running slow.
I buzzed your bell little woman,
Well I hold up my head,
Well I'm just tryin' to make you understand.
Well now ev'rybody tells me.
Somebody HooDoo the HooDoo man.

Well I buzzed your bell this morning,
You had your elevator running slow.
I buzzed your bell little woman,
Well I hold up my head,
Well I'm just tryin' to make you understand.
Well now ev'rybody tells me.
Somebody HooDoo the HooDoo man.

Wonder what's exactly the matter,
Child d'you know the time,
Seemed like an hour.
Ev'rything had changed, but I hold up my head.
Well I'm just tryin' to make you understand.
Well now ev'rybody tells me.
Somebody HooDoo the HooDoo man.

19
I CAN'T HOLD OUT

I just talked to my baby on the telephone, she said:
"Stop what you're doin', baby come on home,
I can't hold out, I can't hold out too long,
I get a real good feelin' talkin' to you on the phone".

You said: "Baby, don't you worry, you're my
heart's desire,
You know that I love you, I can't stand to see you cry,
But I can't hold out, I can't hold out too long,
I get a real good feelin' talkin' to you on the phone."

She said: "Baby you can run, you can walk or fly,
You know that I love you, you're my heart's desire,
I can't hold out, I can't hold out too long,
I get a real good feelin' talkin' to you on the phone."

Talk to me baby, talk to me baby, talk to me baby,
talk to me baby,
I get a real good feelin' talkin' to you on the phone.

WORDS & MUSIC BY ELMORE JAMES.

20
I CAN'T STAND IT

You've been told, so maybe it's time but you learned.
You've been sold, maybe it's time that you earned.
I can't stand it. You're foolin' around. I can't stand it.
You're running around. I won't stand it.
Foolin' around with my heart.

I'll explain, I feel like I'm bein' used.
Make it plain, so you don't get confused.
I can't stand it. Foolin' around. I won't stand it.
You're running around. I can't stand it.
Foolin' around with my heart.

I can't stand it. You're runnin' around. I can't stand it.
You're foolin' around. I can't stand it.
You're playing around with my heart.

It was time, time for me to let you know.
Ain't no crime, no crime to let your feelings show.
I can't stand it. You're runnin' around, I can't stand it.

You're playin' around, I can't stand it.
You're foolin' around, I can't stand it.
You're runnin' around, I can't stand it.
You're playin' around, I can't stand it.

Foolin' around, I can't stand it.
Runnin' around, I can't stand it.
Runnin' around, I won't stand it.
Runnin' around, I won't stand it.

You're foolin' around, I won't stand it.
Playin' around, I won't stand it.
You're runnin' around with my heart.
You're foolin' around with my heart, my heart.
Runnin' around with, foolin' around with my heart.

WORDS & MUSIC BY ERIC CLAPTON.

21
I FEEL FREE

Bum bum bum ba bum bum.
Bum bum bum ba bum bum.
I feel free.
Bum bum bum ba bum bum.
I feel free.

Hmmm hmm hmm hmm hmm hmm hmm.
Hmmm hmm hmm hmm hmm.
Hmmm hmm hmm hmmhmm hmm hmm.
Hmm hmm hmm hmm hm.

Feel when I dance with you.
We move like the sea.
You, you're all I want to know.
I feel free.
I feel free.
I feel free.

Dance floor is like the sea.
Ceiling is the sky.
You're the sun, and as you shine on me,
I feel free.
I feel free.
I feel free.

I can walk down the street, there's no-one there,
Though the pavements are one huge crowd.
I can drive down the road, my eyes don't see,
Though my mind wants to cry out loud.

Ah. Ah. Ah.
I feel free.
I feel free.
I feel free.

I can walk down the street, there's no-one there,
Though the pavements are one huge crowd.
I can drive down the road, my eyes won't see,
Though my mind wants to cry out loud.
Though my mind wants to cry out loud.

Feel when I dance with you.
We move like the sea.
You, you're all I want to know.
I feel free.
I feel free.
I feel free.

Dance floor is like the sea.
Ceiling is the sky.
You're the sun, and as you shine on me,
I feel free.
I feel free.
I feel free.

Ah. Ah.

WORDS & MUSIC BY JACK BRUCE & PETE BROWN.

22
IF I DON'T BE THERE BY MORNING

Blue sky upon the horizon.
Private eye is on my trail.
And if I don't be there by morning,
You know that I must have spent the night in jail.

I been runnin' from Memphis to LA.
Had an appointment set sometime for today.
And if I don't be there by morning,
You know that I must have gone the other way.

Finding my way back to you, girl
Lonely and blue and mistreated too.
Sometimes I think of you, girl.
Is it true that you think of me too?

I got a woman livin' in LA.
I got a woman waitin' for my pay.
And if I don't be there by morning,
Pack my clothes, get down on your knees and pray.

Finding my way back to you, girl
Lonely and blue and mistreated too.
Sometimes I think of you, girl.
Is it true that you think of me too?

I left my woman with a twenty dollar bill.
I left her waiting, I hope she's waiting for me still.
And if I don't be there by morning,
I know that I, I never will.

WORDS & MUSIC BY BOB DYLAN & HELENA SPRINGS.

23
KEY TO THE HIGHWAY

I got the key to the highway, billed out and
bound to go.
I'm gonna leave, yeah, I'm runnin'; walkin' is
much too slow.
I'm goin' back to the border, woman where I'm
better now.
'Cause you hav'n'done nothin', drove a good man away
from home.

As the moon peeks over the mountains, I'll be on
my way.
I'm gonna roam this old highway until the break of day.

I got the key to the highway, billed out and
bound to go.
I'm gonna leave, yeah, I'm runnin'; walkin' is
much too slow.
I'm goin' back to the border, woman where I'm
better now.
'Cause you hav'n'done nothin', drove a good man away
from home.

As the moon peeks over the mountains, I'll be on
my way.
I'm gonna roam this old highway until the break of day.

24
KNOCKIN' ON HEAVEN'S DOOR

Ma, take this badge off of me
I can't use it any more.
It's getting dark, too dark to see.
I feel like I'm knockin' on heaven's door.

Knock, knock knockin' on heaven's door.
Knock, knock knockin' on heaven's door.
Knock, knock knockin' on heaven's door.
Knock, knock knockin' on heaven's door.

Ma take these guns away from me.
I can't shoot them any more.
There's a long black cloud following me.
I feel like I'm knockin' on heaven's door.

Knock, knock knockin' on heaven's door.
Knock, knock knockin' on heaven's door.
Knock, knock knockin' on heaven's door.
Knock, knock knockin' on heaven's door.

Knock, knock knockin' on heaven's door.
Knock, knock knockin' on heaven's door.
Knock, knock knockin' on heaven's door.
Knock, knock knockin' on heaven's door.

25
LAWDY MAMA

Wan'go hoppin' too late at night?
Lawdy mama, no need to worry.
Wan'go hoppin' too late at night?
I got a real funny feelin'
You're gonna treat your Daddy right.

Big leg woman, come and hold my hand.
Lawdy mama, no need to worry.
Big leg woman, come and hold my hand.
I got a real funny feelin'
You wanna love another man.

TRADITIONAL ARRANGED BY ERIC CLAPTON.

26
LAY DOWN SALLY

There is nothing that is wrong in wanting you to stay here with me.
I know you've got somewhere to go, but won't you make yourself at home And stay with me?
And don't you ever leave.
Lay down Sally and rest here in my arms.
Don't you think you want someone to talk to?
Lay down Sally, no need to leave so soon.
I've been trying all night long just to talk to you.

The sun ain't nearly on the rise, and we still got the moon and stars above.
Underneath the velvet skies, love is all that matters;
Won't you stay with me?
And don't you ever leave.
Lay down Sally and rest here in my arms.
Don't you think you want someone to talk to?
Lay down Sally, no need to leave so soon.
I've been trying all night long just to talk to you.

I long to see the morning light colouring your face so dreamily.
So don't you go and say goodbye; you can lay your worries down
And stay with me?
And don't you ever leave.
Lay down Sally and rest here in my arms.
Don't you think you want someone to talk to?
Lay down Sally, no need to leave so soon.
I've been trying all night long just to talk to you.

Lay down Sally and rest here in my arms.
Don't you think you want someone to talk to?
Lay down Sally, no need to leave so soon.
I've been trying all night long just to talk to you.

Lay down Sally and rest here in my arms.
Don't you think you want someone to talk to?
Lay down Sally, no need to leave so soon.
I've been trying all night long just to talk to you.

WORDS & MUSIC BY ERIC CLAPTON, MARCY LEVY & GEORGE TERRY.

27
LAYLA

And what'll you do when you get lonely,
When nobody's waiting by your side?
And you've been running and hiding much too long,
You know it's just your foolish pride.

Layla, you got me on my knees.
Layla, I'm begging darlin' please.
Layla, darlin' won't you ease my worried mind.

Tried to give you consolation,
And your old man won't let you down.
Like a fool I fell in love with you,
And you turned the whole world upside down.

Layla, you got me on my knees.
Layla, I'm begging darlin' please.
Layla, darlin' won't you ease my worried mind.

Let's make the best of the situation,
Before I finally go insane.
Please don't say that we'll never find a way,
And tell me all my love's in vain.

Layla, you got me on my knees.
Layla, I'm begging darlin' please,
Layla, darlin' won't you ease my worried mind.
Layla, you've got me on my knees.
Layla, I'm begging darlin' please,
Layla, darlin' won't you ease my worried mind.

WORDS & MUSIC BY ERIC CLAPTON & JIM GORDON.

28
LONELY STRANGER

I must be invisible.
No-one knows me.
I have crawled down dead end streets
On my hands and knees.

I was born with a raging thirst,
A hunger to be free.
But I've learned through the years,
Don't encourage me.

'Cause I'm a lonely stranger here
Well beyond my day,
But I don't know what's goin' on,
So I'll be on my way.
Yes, I will. Yes, I will. Yes, I will.

When I walk, stay behind,
Don't get close to me,
'Cause it's sure to end in tears,
So just let me be.

Some will say that I'm no good,
Maybe I agree.
Take a look, then walk away,
That's alright with me.

'Cause I'm a lonely stranger here
Well beyond my day,
But I don't know what's goin' on,
So I'll be on my way.
Yes, I will. Yes, I will. Yes, I will.
Yes, I will. Yes, I will.

WORDS & MUSIC BY ERIC CLAPTON.

29
LEAD ME ON

Tell me anything you think I want to hear,
Just to keep me standing here,
To secure your shaky fears.
Tell me you love me but in your heart you know
you don't,
So you lie 'cause you think I want
To make believe you love when you don't.

Lead me on. Lead me on. Lead me on. Lead me on.
I'll play along and along and along,
Baby lead me on. Lead me on.

Pretend it's raining when the tears fall from my eyes,
And you're warm when you're cold as ice,
And everything's gonna be alright.
And it's a shame little Johnny wears my name,
And you know I'm not the one,
Still you say he is my son.

Lead me on. Lead me on. Lead me on. Lead me on.
I'll play along and along and along,
Baby lead me on. Lead me on.

And when I leave to go to work for you,
You cry you're lonely too,
To make me feel your love is true.
But in your dreams you slip and tell it all,
I hear you calling out his name,
You say you love him loud and plain.

Lead me on. Lead me on. Lead me on. Lead me on.
I'll play along and along and along,
Baby lead me on. Lead me on.
Lead me on. Lead me on.

30
LET IT GROW

Standing at the crossroads tryin' to read the signs
To tell me which way I should go to find the answer
And all the time I know,
Plant your love and let it grow.

Let it grow, let it grow,
Let it blossom let it flow.
In the sun, the rain, the snow,
Love is lovely, let it grow.

Looking for a reason to check out on my mind,
Trying hard to get a friend that I can count on,
But there's nothing left to show,
Plant your love and let it grow.

Let it grow, let it grow,
Let it blossom let it flow.
In the sun, the rain, the snow,
Love is lovely, let it grow.

Time is getting shorter, there's much for you to do,
Only ask and you will get what you are needing,
The rest is up to you,
Plant your love and let it grow.

Let it grow, let it grow,
Let it blossom let it flow.
In the sun, the rain, the snow,
Love is lovely, let it grow.

31
MAINLINE FLORIDA

My heart was leaping in the sun,
My friends all say that you're the one.
Let me get this one thing very clear,
There ain't enough going on down here.
Mainline Florida, oh say,
Mainline Florida, okay.

Here arms were open, open wide,
Her invitation's a changing tide.
I could remember not long ago,
We took a cruise down on hotel row.
Mainline Florida, oh say,
Mainline Florida, okay.

32
MEAN OLD FRISCO

Well, that mean old dirty 'Frisco, and that low down
Santa Fe,
Mean old 'Frisco and that low down Santa Fe.
Well, take my gal away, Lord, and go back out on me.

Well my mama, she done told me and my papa told
me too,
Mama told me, and my papa told me too.
Woman get in your face, son, she ain't no friend
to you.

Well, I'm goin' 'way now, baby, and your cryin' won't
make me stay,
Goin' 'way, baby, and your cryin' won't make
me stay.
Well, the more you cry, little girl, drive me away.

Well, that mean old dirty 'Frisco, and that low down
Santa Fe,
Mean old 'Frisco and that low down Santa Fe.
Well, take my gal away, Lord, and go back out on me.

33
MOTHERLESS CHILDREN

Motherless children have a hard time when your
mother is dead, Lord.
Motherless children have a hard time when your
mother is dead, Lord.
They don't have anywhere to go, wandering 'round
from door to door.
Nobody can treat you like a mother will when your
mother is dead, Lord.

Father will do the best he can when your mother is
dead, Lord.
Father will do the best he can when your mother is
dead, Lord.
Father will do the best he can, so many things a father
can't understand.
Nobody treats you like a mother will when your
mother is dead, Lord.

Sister will do the best she can when your mother is
dead, Lord.
Sister will do the best she can when your mother is
dead, Lord.
Sister will do the best she can, so many things a sister
can't understand.
Nobody treats you like a mother will when your
mother is dead, Lord.

When your mother is dead, when your mother is dead.
When your mother is dead, Lord, when your mother
is dead.

TRADITIONAL.
ARRANGED BY ERIC CLAPTON & CARL RADLE.

34
PLEASE BE WITH ME

On my word, what does it mean?
Is it love or is it me
That makes me change so suddenly
From lookin' out to feelin' free?

I sit here lyin' in my bed,
Wondrin' what it was I'd said
That made me think
I'd lost my head
When I knew I'd lost my heart instead.

So won't you please read my signs?
By a gypsy. Tell me what I hope to find
Deep within me,
Because you can find my mind, please be with me.

Of all the better things I've heard,
Lovin' you has made the words
And all the rest seem so absurd,
'Cause in the end it all comes out, I'm sure.

Won't you please read my signs?
By a gypsy. Tell me what I hope to find
Deep within me,
Because you can find my mind, please be with me.

WORDS & MUSIC BY CHARLES SCOTT BOYER.

35
NO ALIBIS

I beg your pardon, hello darlin',
This is me you're talkin' to,
Sit down and tell me about it,
You don't have to shout it at me,
Tell me what you really want to do.

Don't give me no alibis,
No untrue stories trying to justify,
Don't want no alibis,
Just another reason for another lie.

And it gets steeper, the hole you dig gets deeper,
You better stop and climb out,
Trying to give it all to you,
Baby, I can see right through you,
Sometimes you lose what it's all about.

Don't give me no alibis,
No untrue stories trying to justify,
Don't want no alibis,
Just another reason for another lie.

Mountain gets steeper, the hole you dig is
getting deeper,
You better reach and pull yourself out,
No-one's ever gonna love you,
The way that I love you,
I never wanna to see you doin' without.

Don't give me no alibis,
No untrue stories trying to justify,
Don't want no alibis,
Just another reason for another lie.

Don't give me no alibis,
No untrue stories trying to justify,
Don't want no alibis,
Just another reason for another lie.

WORDS & MUSIC BY JERRY LYNN WILLIAMS.

36
NOBODY KNOWS YOU WHEN YOU'RE DOWN AND OUT

Once I lived the life of a millionaire.
Spent all my money, I just did not care.
Took all my friends out for a good time,
Bought bootleg whiskey, champagne and wine.
Then I began to fall so low.
Lost all my good friends,
I did not have nowhere to go.
I get my hands on a dollar again,
I'm gonna hang on to it till that eagle grins, yeah.

No, no nobody knows you when you're down and out.
In your pocket, not one penny.
And as for friends, you don't have any.
When you fin'lly get back up on your feet again,
Everybody wants to be your long lost friend.
Said, it's mighty strange, 'out a doubt.
Nobody knows you when you're down and out, yeah.

And when you fin'lly get back up on your feet again,
Everybody wants to be your good old long lost friend.
Said, it's mighty strange, yeah.
Nobody knows you, nobody knows,
Nobody knows you when you're down and out.

WORDS & MUSIC BY JIMMIE COX.

37
OLD LOVE

I can feel your body when I'm lying in my bed.
Too much confusion goin' round through my head.
Makes me so angry to know that the flame still burns.
Why can't I get over? When will I ever learn?
Old love leave me alone.
Old love go on home.

I can see your face, but I know that it's not real,
Just an illusion caused by how I used to feel.
Makes me so angry to know that the flame still burns.
Why can't I get over? When will I ever learn?
Old love leave me alone.
Old love go on home.

Old love leave me alone.
Old love go on home.

WORDS & MUSIC BY ERIC CLAPTON & ROBERT CRAY.

38
ONE MORE CHANCE

Give me one more chance to make it up to you.
Give me one more chance to show what I can do.
Let me prove to you that my love is strong.
Won't you come back home that's where you belong.

Oh baby, won't you give me one more chance?
Won't you give me one more chance?

Well the sun won't shine and it refused to rain
And I banged my head, but I feel no pain.
When I tell myself that I could start anew,
But I know darn well it all depends on you.

Oh baby, won't you give me one more chance?
Won't you give me one more chance?

So if you hear me say do not change your mind
And give a thought to me, I won't be hard to find.
And I promise you I'll do the best I can.
Can my evil ways, and be your lovin' man.

Oh baby, won't you give me one more chance?
Won't you give me one more chance?

So, give me one more chance to make it up to you.
Give me one more chance to show what I can do.
Let me prove to you that my love is strong.
Won't you come back home that's where you belong.

Oh baby, won't you give me one more chance?
Won't you give me one more chance.
Won't you give me one more chance.

WORDS & MUSIC BY ERIC CLAPTON.

39
PRESENCE OF THE LORD

I have fin'ly found a way to live
Just like I never could before.
I know that I don't have much to give.
But I can open any door.
Ev'rybody knows the secret,
Ev'rybody knows the score.
I have fin'ly found a way to live
In the colour of the Lord.

I have fin'ly found a place to live
Just like I never could before.
And I know I don't have much to give.
But soon I'll open any door.
Ev'rybody knows the secret,
Ev'rybody knows the score.
I have fin'ly found a place to live
In the presence of the Lord.

I have fin'ly found a way to live
Just like I never could before.
I know that I don't have much to give.
But I can open any door.
Ev'rybody knows the secret,
Ev'rybody knows the score.
I have fin'ly found a way to live
In the colour of the Lord.

WORDS & MUSIC BY ERIC CLAPTON.

40
PRETENDING

How many times must we tell the tale?
How many times must we fail?
Living in a lost memory you just recalled.

Working on the sound of the band, trying to get the
music right,
Two go out working, three stay home at night.

That's when she said she was pretending, like she knew
the plan,
That's when I knew she was pretending,
pretending to understand.
Pretending. Pretending. Pretending. Pretending.

Satisfied but lost in love, situations change,
You're never who you used to think you are,
how strange.

That's when she said she was pretending, like she knew
the plan,
That's when I knew she was pretending,
pretending to understand.
Pretending. Pretending. Pretending. Pretending.

I get lost in alibis, sadness can't prevail,
Everybody knows strong love can't fail.

Don't be pretending 'bout how you feel.
Don't be pretending your love is real.
Don't be pretending 'bout how you feel.
Don't be pretending your love is real.
Pretending. Pretending. Pretending. Pretending.

WORDS & MUSIC BY JERRY LYNN WILLIAMS.

41
ROLL IT OVER

Go down easy and let me take my time.
Go down easy and let me take my time.
Rock me slow till I lose my mind.

Roll it over, let's take it from behind.
Roll it over, let's take it from behind.
S'only love, God knows it ain't no crime.

You don't know how much it means
To be here in your arms.
Roll it over. Roll it over.

Go down easy and let me take my time.
Go down easy and let me take my time.
Rock me slow till I lose my mind.

Roll it over, let's take it from behind.
Roll it over, let's take it from behind.
S'only love, God knows it ain't no crime.

You don't know how much it means
To be here in your arms.
Roll it over. Roll it over.

WORDS & MUSIC BY ERIC CLAPTON & BOBBY WHITLOCK.

42
RAMBLIN' ON MY MIND

I've got ramblin', I've got ramblin' all on my mind.
I've got ramblin', I've got ramblin' all on my mind.
Is to leave my baby, 'cause she treat me so unkind.

I'm goin' down to the station, catch that old fast milk train, you'll see.
I'm goin' down to the station, catch that old fast milk train, you'll see.
I've got the blues 'bout Miss So and So, and the sun got the blues 'bout me.

I got mean things, I've got mean things all on my mind,
Little girl, little girl, I've got mean things all on my mind.
Is to leave my baby, 'cause she treat me so unkind.

WORDS & MUSIC BY ROBERT JOHNSON.
ARRANGED BY ERIC CLAPTON.

43
ROLLIN' AND TUMBLIN'

Well, I woke up this mornin', I best get rollin' on.

Well, now come here baby, sit down on daddy's knee.
Well, now come here baby, sit down on daddy's knee.
I wanna tell you about the way they treated me.

Well, I rolled and I tumbled, cried the whole
night long.
Well, I rolled and I tumbled, cried the whole
night long.
When I woke up this mornin', all I had was gone.

WORDS & MUSIC BY MUDDY WATERS.

44
RUNNING ON FAITH

Lately I've been running on faith,
What else can a poor boy do?
But my world will be right,
When love comes over you.

Lately I've been talking in my sleep,
Can't imagine what I'd have to say,
Except my world will be right,
When love comes back your way.

I've always been one to take each and every day,
Seems like by now I've found a love who cares just
for me.

Then we'd go running on faith,
All of our dreams will come true
And our world will be right,
When love comes over me and you.

I've always been one to take each and every day,
Seems like by now I've found a love who cares just
for me.

Then we'd go running on faith,
All of our dreams will come true
All the world will be right,
When love comes over you.
When loves comes over you.
When loves comes over you.

WORDS & MUSIC BY JERRY LYNN WILLIAMS.

45
TALES OF BRAVE ULYSSES

You thought the leaden winter would bring you
down forever,
But you rode upon a steamer to the violence of the sun.

And the colours of the sea blind your eyes with
trembling mermaids,
And you touch the distant beaches with tales of
brave Ulysses;
How his naked ears were tortured by the sirens
sweetly singing,
For the sparkling waves are calling you to kiss their
white laced lips.

And you see a girl's brown body dancing through
the turquoise,
And her footprints make you follow where the sky
loves the sea;
And when your fingers find her she drowns you in
her body,
Carving deep blue ripples in the tissues of your mind.

Tiny purple fishes run laughing through your fingers,
And you want to take her with you to the hard land of
the winter.
Her name is Aphrodite and she rides a crimson shell.
And you know you cannot leave her, for you touched
the distant sands
With tales of brave Ulysses; how his naked ears were
tortured by the
Sirens sweetly singin'.

And the tiny purple fishes run laughing through
your fingers,
And you want to take her with you to the hard land of
the winter.

WORDS & MUSIC BY ERIC CLAPTON & MARTIN SHARP.

46
SPOONFUL

Could fill a spoonsful of diamonds, could fill a
spoonsful of gold.
Just a little spoon of your precious love satisfy my soul.
Man lies about it; some of them cries about it.
Some of them dies about it. Ev'rything's a-fightin'
about the spoonful.
That spoon, that spoon, that spoonful.
That spoon, that spoon, that spoonful.
That spoon, that spoon, that spoonful.
That spoon, that spoon, that spoon.

Could fill a spoonsful of coffee; could fill a spoonsful
of tea.
Just a little spoon of your precious love, is that enough
for me?
Men lies about it. Some of them cries about it.
Some of them dies about it. Ev'rything's a-fightin'
about the spoonful.
That spoon, that spoon, that spoonful.
That spoon, that spoon, that spoonful.
That spoon, that spoon, that spoonful.
That spoon, that spoon, hey.

Could fill a spoonsful of water, saved them from the
desert sands.
Was a little spoon of your love, baby, saved you from
another man.
Men lies a some of them cried about it.
Some of them dies. Ev'rything's a-fightin' about it, uh
Ev'rything's a-cryin' about it, uh
Ev'rything's a, ev'rything's a-dyin' about it.
Ev'rything's a-cryin' about it. Ev'rything's a-lyin'
about it.
Lit'l' old, lit'l' old, spoonful, spoonful, Hey!
Ev'rything's dyin' about it, uh.
Alright, just cryin' about it.

That spoon, that spoon, that little old spoon,
Little old spoon, little old little old spoon,
Little old spoon, little old spoonful.
That spoon, that spoon, that spoonful.
Spoon, that spoon, that spoonful. Yeah.
Ev'rything's a-dyin' about it. Hey!

WORDS & MUSIC BY WILLIE DIXON.

47
STEADY ROLLIN' MAN

I am a steady rollin' man and I roll both night and day,
I am a steady rollin' man and I roll both night and day,
But I ain't got no sweet woman, ooh Lord, to be rollin' this-a way.

I am a man that rolls when icicles are hangin' on the trees,
I am a man that rolls when icicles are hangin' on the trees,
But can't you hear me beggin', mama, ooh Lord, down on my bended knee.

I am a steady rollin' man and I roll both night and day,
I am a steady rollin' man and I roll both night and day,
But I ain't got no sweet woman, ooh Lord, to be rollin' this-a way.

WORDS & MUSIC BY ROBERT JOHNSON.
ARRANGED BY ERIC CLAPTON.

48
STRANGE BREW

Strange brew, killin' what's inside of you.
She's a witch of trouble in electric blue.
In her own mad mind she's in love with you, with you.
Now what you gonna do?
Strange brew, killin' what's inside of you.

She's some kind of demon messin' in the glue.
If you don't watch out, it'll stick to you.
What kind of fool are you?
Strange brew, killin' what's inside of you.

On a boat in the middle of the raging sea,
She would make a scene for it all to be ignored,
And wouldn't you be bored.
Strange brew, killin' what's inside of you.

Strange brew, strange brew, strange brew, strange brew,
Strange brew, killin' what's inside of you.

WORDS & MUSIC BY ERIC CLAPTON, MIKE COLLINS & FELIX PAPPALARDI.

49
SUNSHINE OF YOUR LOVE

It's getting near dawn, when lights close their
tired eyes.
I'll soon be with you, my love, to give you my
dawn surprise.
I'll be with you, darling, soon.
I'll be with you when the stars start falling.

I've been waiting so long to be where I'm going
In the sunshine of your love.

I'm with you, my love; the light shining through
on you.
Yes I'm with you, my love. It's the morning and just
we two.
I'll stay with you, darling, now.
I'll stay with you 'til my seeds are dried up.

I've been waiting so long to be where I'm going
In the sunshine of your love.

I'm with you, my love; the light shining through
on you.
Yes I'm with you, my love. It's the morning and just
we two.
I'll stay with you, darling, now.
I'll stay with you 'til my seeds are dried up.

I've been waiting so long to be where I'm going
In the sunshine of your love.

WORDS & MUSIC BY JACK BRUCE, PETE BROWN & ERIC CLAPTON.

50
TEARS IN HEAVEN

Would you know my name if I saw you in heaven?
Would it be the same if I saw you in heaven?
I must be strong and carry on,
'Cause I know I don't belong here in heaven.

Would you hold my hand if I saw you in heaven?
Would you help me stand if I saw you in heaven?
I'll find my way through night and day
'Cause I know I just can't stay here in heaven.

Time can bring you down, time can bend your knees.
Time can break your heart have you beggin' please,
beggin' please.
Beyond the door there's peace, I'm sure,
And I know there'll be no more tears in heaven.

Would you know my name if I saw you in heaven?
Would it be the same if I saw you in heaven?
I must be strong and carry on,
'Cause I know I don't belong here in heaven.
'Cause I know I don't belong here in heaven.

WORDS & MUSIC BY ERIC CLAPTON & WILL JENNINGS.

51
TELL THE TRUTH

Tell the truth.
Tell me, who's been foolin' you?
Tell the truth.
Who's been foolin' who?

There you sit there, lookin' so cool,
While the whole show is passin' you by.
Better come to terms with your fellow men soon
'Cause the whole world is shakin' now.
Can't you feel it?
A new dawn is breakin' now.
Can't you see it?

Tell the truth.
Tell me, who's been foolin' you?
Tell the truth.
Who's been foolin' who?

It doesn't matter just who you are,
Or where you're goin' or been.
Open your eyes and look into your heart;
The whole world is shakin' now.
Can't you feel it?
A new dawn is breakin' now.
Can't you see it?
Can't you see it?
Yeah. I can see it.
I can see it
Yeah! I can see it, I can see it. Yeah.

Tell the truth.
Tell me, who's been foolin' you?
Tell the truth.
Who's been foolin' who?

Hear what I say 'cause ev'ry word is true.
You know I wouldn't tell you no lies.
Your time's comin'.
Gonna be soon, boy:
The whole world is shakin' now.
Can't you feel it?
A new dawn is breakin' now.
Can't you see it?
Can't you see it?
Yeah. I can see it.
I can see it
Yeah! I can see it, I can see it. Yeah.

Can't you see it?
Can't you see it? Yeah.
Wou, wou, wou, wou,
The whole world is shakin' now.
Can't you feel it?
A new dawn is breakin' now, can't you see it?
Can't you see it? Yeah!
I can see it,
I can see it. Yeah!
I can see it.
I can see it, Yeah!
I can see it.
I can see it, Yeah!

WORDS & MUSIC BY ERIC CLAPTON & BOBBY WHITLOCK.

52
TOO BAD

It's too bad I don't love you,
For you have worried me night and day.
It's too bad I don't love you,
For you have worried me night and day.
'Til my heart begins to stammer
And my hair is turning grey.

It's too bad I don't need you,
'Cause we get along so good.
It's too bad I don't need you,
Because we get along so good.
You must be thinking 'bout this time,
That my poor heart is made of wood.

It's too bad I don't miss you,
'Cause you are always on my mind.
It's too bad I don't miss you,
'Cause you are always on my mind.
I want to stay around, li'l' silly girl,
And learn to love you all the time.

WORDS & MUSIC BY ERIC CLAPTON.

53
THE SHAPE YOU'RE IN

I took my baby to see a show.
She was tellin' me she didn't wanna go.
I said "Come on, girl, what's the matter with you?"
But I could tell by the smell that she'd had a few.

A-hold on, baby, don't you get too tight.
You started early and we've got all night.
You gotta take it easy, take it slow.
We don't want the whole world to know about the
shape you're in.
Hey babe, the shape you're in, about the shape
you're in.
Hey, girl the shape you're in.

My little girl really loves that wine.
Wine will do it to her almost ev'ry time.
If it's red or white, if it's in between,
She can drink more wine than I've ever seen.

I sing, hold on, girl, don't get too tight.
You started early and we've got all night.
You gotta take it easy, take it slow.
We don't want the whole world to know about the
shape you're in.
Hey babe, the shape you're in, about the shape
you're in.
Hey, girl the shape you're in.

I'm not tryin' to get heavy with you.
I'll mind my own bus'ness if you want me to.
But I love you, girl I don't love no-one else.
I'm just tellin' you, baby, 'cause I've been there
myself.

I sing, hold on, girl, don't get too tight.
You started early and we've got all night.
You gotta take it easy, take it slow.
We don't want the whole world to know about the
shape you're in.
Hey babe, the shape you're in, about the shape
you're in.
Hey, girl the shape you're in, about the shape
you're in.
Hey babe, the shape you're in, about the shape
you're in.
Come on, girl the shape you're in.

WORDS & MUSIC BY ERIC CLAPTON.

54
WATCH YOURSELF

You better watch yourself,
You better watch yourself,
You better watch yourself,
I got my eye on you.

You steal my love
And go away,
Don't tell me you'll see me
Another day.
You better watch yourself,
You better watch yourself,
You better watch yourself.
I got my eye on you. Yeah!

You gone and left me,
Left me here to cry,
Y'know I love
A-you know you're my desire.
Watch yourself,
You better watch yourself,
You better watch yourself,
I got my eye on you.

I gave you all my love,
Everything too.
A fine Cadillac,
Tell me what you're gonna do.
You better watch yourself,
You better watch yourself,
You better watch yourself.
I got my eye on you.

People all talkin'
All over town.
Sayin' you don't love me,
And you're gonna put me down.
You better watch yourself,
You better watch yourself,
You better watch yourself.
I got my eye on you.

Tell me what's the matter,
What you gonna do.
You say you're gonna quit me
Then you say we're through.
You better watch yourself,
You better watch yourself,
You better watch yourself.
You better watch yourself,
You better watch yourself,
I got my eyes on you.

WORDS & MUSIC BY BUDDY GUY.

55
WHITE ROOM

In a white room with black curtains near the station.
Black roof country, no gold pavements, tired starlings.
Silver horses ran down moonbeams in your dark eyes.
Dawnlight smiles on you leaving, my contentment.

I'll wait in this place where the sun never shines;
Wait in this place where the shadows run from
themselves.
You said no strings could secure you at the station.
Platform ticket, restless diesels, goodbye windows.

I walked into such a sad time at the station.
As I walked out, felt my own need just beginning.
I'll wait in the queue when the trains come back;
Lie with you where the shadows run from themselves.

At the party she was kindness in the hard crowd;
Consolation for the old wound now forgotten.
Yellow tigers crouched in jungles in the dark eyes.
She's just dressing, goodbye windows, tired starlings.
I'll sleep in this place with the lonely crowd,
Life in the dark where the shadows run
from themselves.

WORDS & MUSIC BY JACK BRUCE & PETE BROWN.

56
WHY DOES LOVE GOT TO BE SO SAD?

Got to find me a way
Take me back to yesterday.
How can I ever hope to forget you?
Won't you show me a place
Where I can hide my lonely face?
I know you're gonna break my heart if I let you.

Why does love got to be so sad?
Why does love got to be so sad?
Why does love got to be so sad?
Why does love got to be so sad?

Like a moth to a flame,
Like a song without a name,
I've never been the same since I met you.
Like a bird on the wing
I've got a brand new song to sing.
Can't keep from singing about you.

Why does love got to be so sad?
Why does love got to be so sad?
Why does love got to be so sad?
Why does love got to be so sad?

I'm beginning to see
What a fool you've made of me.
I might break the law when I find you.
Stop running away
I've got a better game to play.
You know I can't go on without you.

Why does love got to be so sad?
Why does love got to be so sad?
Why does love got to be so sad?
Why does love got to be so sad?

Why does love got to be so sad?
Why does love got to be so sad?
Why does love got to be so sad?
Why does love got to be so sad?

WORDS & MUSIC BY ERIC CLAPTON & BOBBY WHITLOCK.

57
WONDERFUL TONIGHT

It's late in the evening, she's wond'ring what clothes
to wear.
She puts on her make-up and brushes her long
blonde hair.
And then she asks me, "Do I look alright?"
And I say, "Yes, you look wonderful tonight."

We go to a party, and ev'ry one turns to see
This beautiful lady is walking around with me.
And then she asks me, "Do you feel alright?"
And I say, "Yes I feel wonderful tonight."

I feel wonderful because I see the love light in
your eyes.
Then the wonder of it all is that you just don't realize
How much I love you.

It's time to go home now, and I've got an aching head.
So I give her the car keys, and she helps me to bed.
And then I tell her, as I turn out the light,
I say, "My darling, you are wonderful tonight."

Oh my darling, you are wonderful tonight.

WORDS & MUSIC BY ERIC CLAPTON.

58
WORRIED LIFE BLUES

Oh! Lordy Lord, Oh! Lordy Lord,
It hurts me so bad for us to part,
But someday babe,
I ain't gonna worry my life any more.

You're on my mind, ev'ry place I go,
And how much I love you nobody knows
But someday babe,
I ain't gonna worry my life any more.

So many days, since you went away,
I've had to worry, both night and day.
But some day babe,
I ain't gonna worry my life any more.

So many nights, since you've been gone,
I've been worried and leaving my life alone.
But some day babe,
I ain't gonna worry my life any more.

So that's my story, and this is all I have to say to you,
Goodbye babe, I don't care what you do.
'Cause someday babe,
Lord I ain't gonna worry my life any more.

Oh! Lordy Lord, Oh! Lordy Lord,
It hurt me so bad, for us to part,
But some day babe,
I ain't gonna worry my life any more.

WORDS & MUSIC BY MACEO MERRIWEATHER.

THE MUSIC

1
ALBERTA

WORDS & MUSIC BY HUDDIE LEDBETTER.

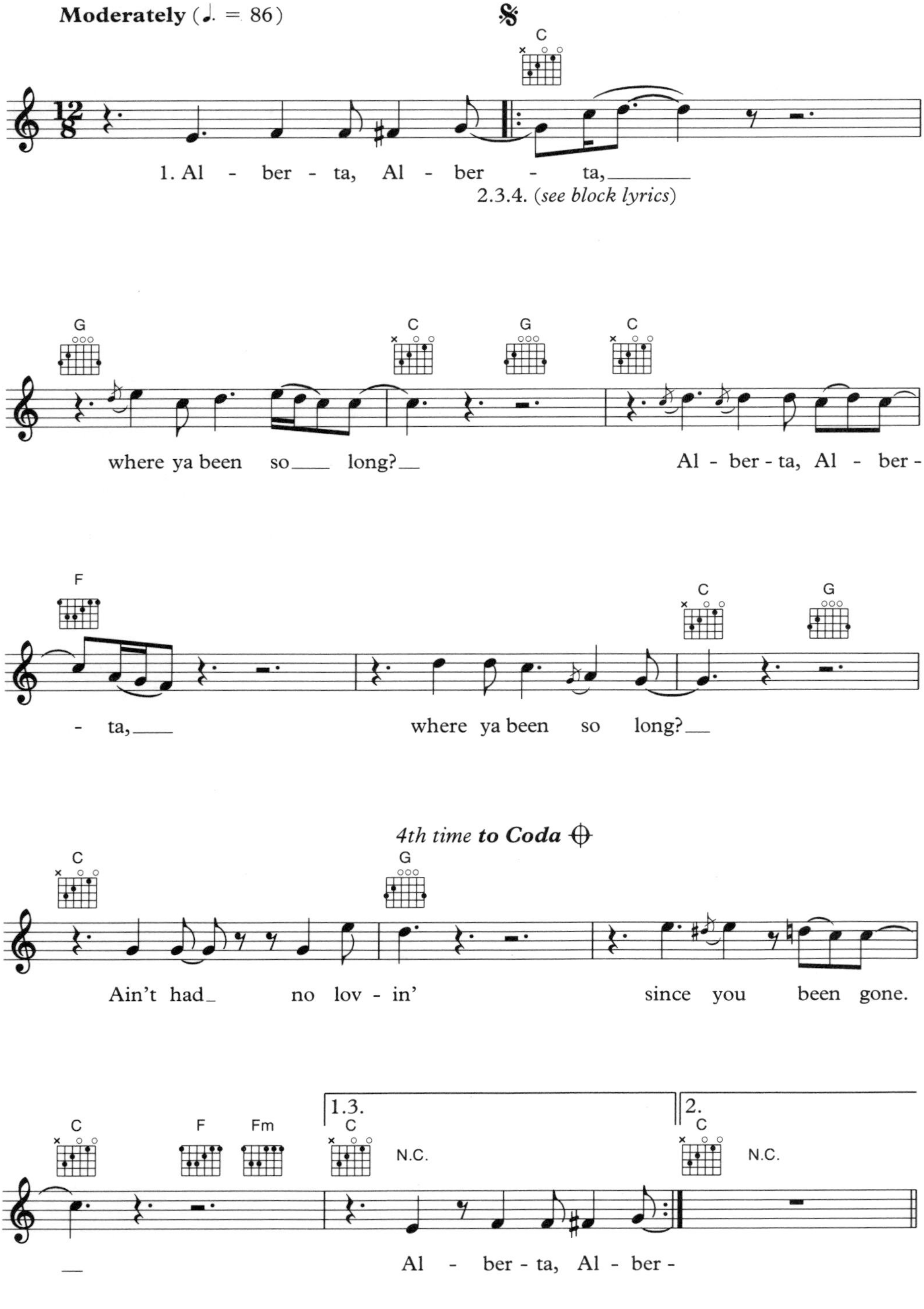

2. Alberta, Alberta, where'd you stay last night?
Alberta, Alberta, where'd you stay last night?
Come home this mornin', clothes don't fit you right.

3. Alberta, Alberta, girl you're on my mind.
Alberta, Alberta, girl you're on my mind.
Ain't had no lovin' in such a great, long time.

4. Alberta, Alberta, where you been so long?
Alberta, Alberta, where you been so long?
Ain't had no lovin' since you've been gone.

ANYTHING FOR YOUR LOVE

WORDS & MUSIC BY JERRY LYNN WILLIAMS.

1.
B♭5 C5 B♭5 C5 B♭5 C5 B♭5 C5
for your love.
2.
B♭5 C5 D5 E♭5 F5 C5 D5 C5
D5 C5 D5 E♭5 F5 C5 D5 C5
D5 E♭ F
I'd do a - ny - thing, a - ny - thing you can dream of,
C5 D5 E♭
I'd do a - ny - thing, a - ny -
F B♭5 C5 B♭5 C5
- thing for your love, for your love,
repeat ad lib. to fade
B♭5 C5 B♭5 C5 B♭5 C5 B♭5 C5
for your love, for your love,
3fr
5fr
6fr
8fr

3

AFTER MIDNIGHT

WORDS & MUSIC BY J.J. CALE.

BADGE

WORDS & MUSIC BY ERIC CLAPTON & GEORGE HARRISON.

Am D Em(add 9)
I told you 'bout the swans, that they live in the park.
Em C Am
Then I told you 'bout our kid, now he's mar-ried to Ma -
Bm Am(add 9) 5fr D Cmaj7 G/B G D Cmaj7 G/B G
- bel.
D Cmaj7 G D Cmaj7
Yes, I told you that the light goes up and down. Don't you no -
G/B G D Cmaj7 G/B G
- tice how the wheel goes 'round. And you bet - ter pick your-self up

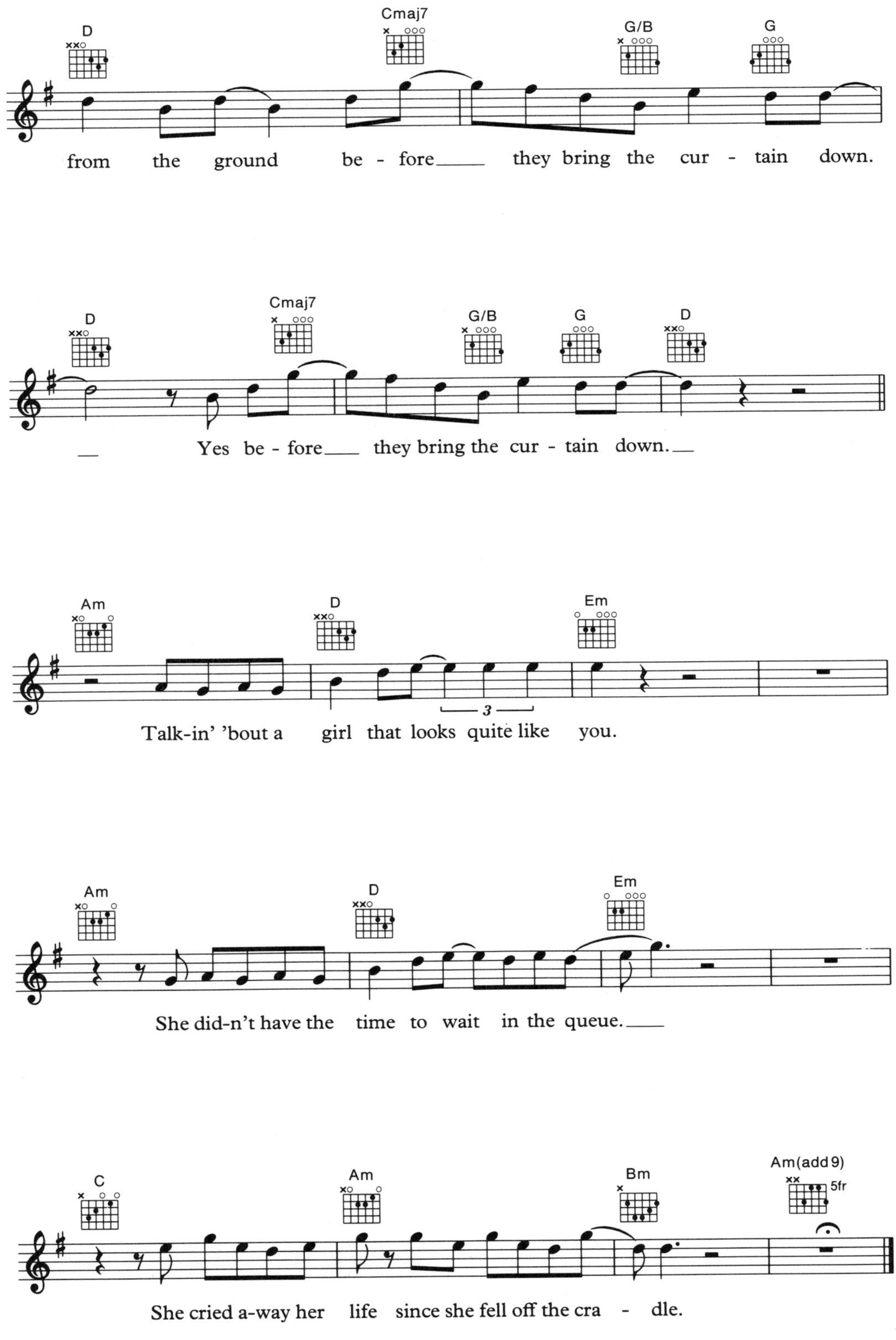
D Cmaj7 G/B G
from the ground be - fore___ they bring the cur - tain down.
D Cmaj7 G/B G D
___ Yes be - fore___ they bring the cur - tain down.___
Am D Em
Talk-in' 'bout a girl that looks quite like you.
3
Am D Em
She did-n't have the time to wait in the queue.___
C Am Bm Am(add 9)
5fr
She cried a-way her life since she fell off the cra - dle.

5

BAD LOVE

WORDS & MUSIC BY ERIC CLAPTON & MICK JONES.

Dm C Dm B♭ C
long. Now I know that I'm one of the
side. And there's no more me - mo - ries
Am B♭ Gm C
luck - y peo - ple, your love is mak - ing me
to re - mind me, your love will keep me a -
G5 Dm C Gm
strong. Had e - nough bad love, I need
live.
Dm C Gm Dm C
some-thing I can be proud of. Had e - nough bad
Gm Dm C B♭
love, no more bad love.
Dm C Gm Dm C Gm
Instrumental
repeat chorus to fade
Dm C Gm Dm C B♭

BEFORE YOU ACCUSE ME

WORDS & MUSIC BY EUGENE MCDANIELS.

E7
A7
I called your ma-ma
E7
'bout three or four nights a - go.
B7
Well, your ma - ma said "Son don't
A7
E7
B7
call my daugh - ter no more."
3. Be -
E7
A7
- fore you 'cuse me, take a look at your -
E7
D♯7
E7
A7
- self.
Be - fore you 'cuse me
E7
take a look at your - self.

B7
You say I'm spend-in' my mon-ey on oth-er wo-men,
A7
E7
you tak-in' mon-ey from some-one else.
(Instrumental)
B7
E7
4. Come on back home, ba-by,
A7
E7
try my love one more time.
A7
Come on back home, ba-by,
E7
try my love one more time.
You know if things
B7
A7
don't go to suit you,
I think I'll lose my mind.

E7
B7
E7
5. Before you 'cuse me,
A7
E7
take a look at yourself.
Be-
A7
E7
-fore you 'cuse me,
take a look at yourself.
B7
You say I'm spendin' my money on other women,
A7
E7
you're takin' money from someone else.
B7
E7
A7
E7
A7
Instrumental
E7
B7
A7
N.C.
D♯9
5fr
E9
6fr

BELL BOTTOM BLUES

WORDS & MUSIC BY ERIC CLAPTON.

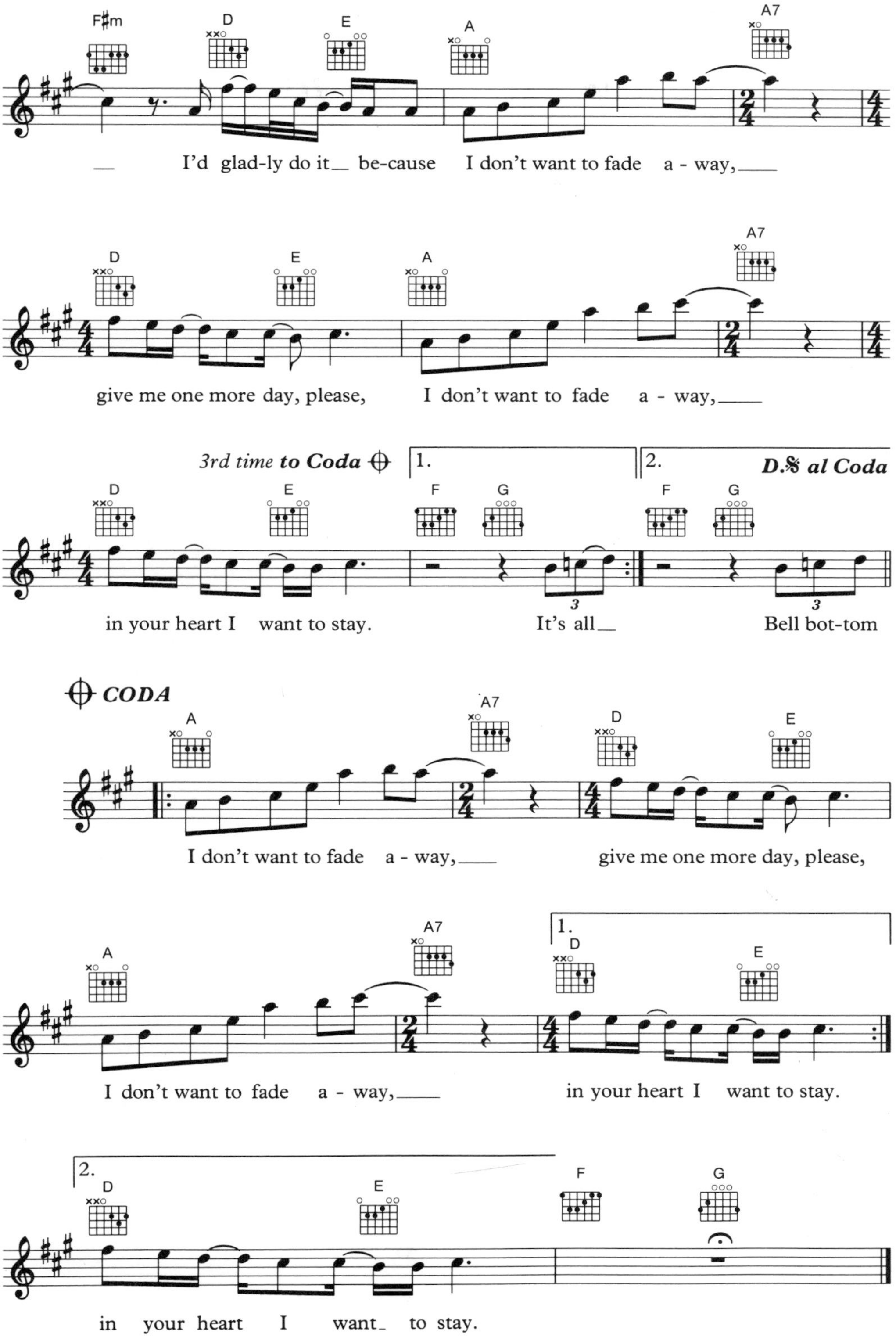
F♯m D E A A7
I'd glad-ly do it because I don't want to fade a-way,
D E A A7
give me one more day, please, I don't want to fade a-way,
3rd time to Coda
1.
2.
D.% al Coda
D E F G F G
in your heart I want to stay. It's all Bell bot-tom
CODA
A A7 D E
I don't want to fade a-way, give me one more day, please,
A A7
1.
D E
I don't want to fade a-way, in your heart I want to stay.
2.
D E F G
in your heart I want to stay.

BETTER MAKE IT THROUGH TODAY

WORDS & MUSIC BY ERIC CLAPTON.

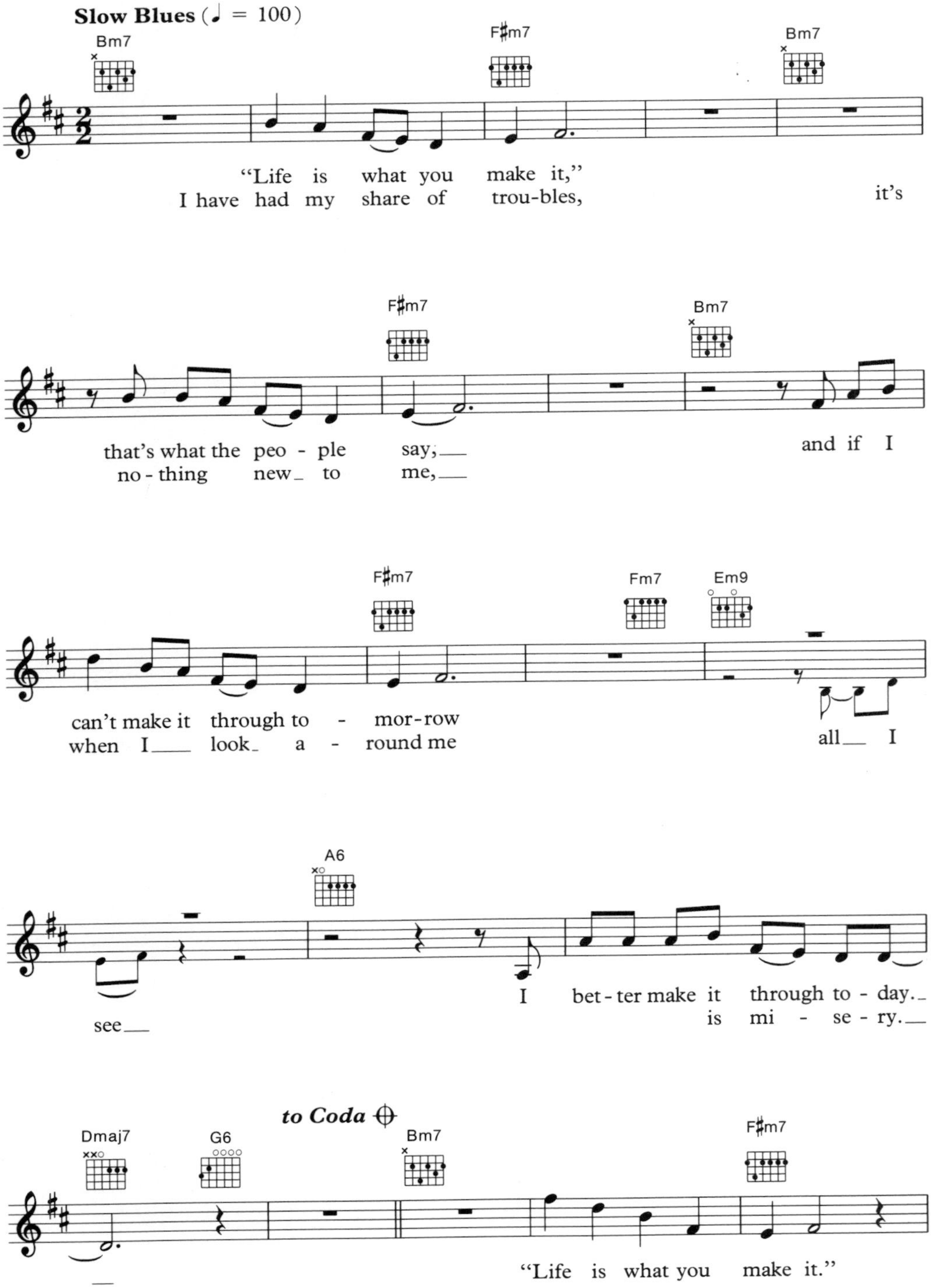

Bm7
F♯m7
at least that's what the peo-ple say,
Bm7
and if we can't make it through to - mor -
F♯m7
Fm7
Em9
A6
- row
we
Dmaj7
G6
bet-ter make it through to - day.
Through to - day.
Dmaj7
G6
Dmaj7
G6
Dmaj7
G6
Through to-day.
D.C. al Coda
CODA
Dmaj7
G6
Dmaj7
G6
Em9

9

BLUES POWER

WORDS & MUSIC BY ERIC CLAPTON & LEON RUSSELL.

F7
now I'm gon-na let you know:
I'm gon-na
C
keep on rock-in', no mat-ter if it's fast or slow.
D7
Ain't gon-na stop un-til the twen-ty-fifth hour,
G7
C
'cause now I'm liv-in' on blues pow-ow-er.
D7
F7
D7
G7
D.C. al Coda
Well I
CODA
repeat to fade
F7
C7
Instrumental ad lib.

CAN'T FIND MY WAY HOME

WORDS & MUSIC BY STEVE WINWOOD.

G
D
-bo - dy holds the key. Well I'm
G/B
Asus4
A
wea - ry and I just ain't got the time,
D
Em
G
and I'm wast - ed and I can't find
to Coda
D/F♯
A
D
D.𝄋 al Coda
my way home. Come
CODA
D
home.
D/C
G/B
Gm/B♭
D/A
Oooh, but I
F
G
D
can't find my way home.
repeat 4 times
with vocal ad lib.

11
COCAINE

WORDS & MUSIC BY J.J. CALE.

2.
E D E D
If your thing is gone, and ya wan-na ride on, co - caine.
E D E D E D E D
— Don't for - get this fact, can't
E D E D
— get back, — co - caine. —
E D C B
She don't lie, — she don't lie, — she don't lie, — co - caine.
E D E D E D E D
—
E D C B
She don't lie, — she don't lie, — she don't lie, — co - caine.
E D E D E D E D
—
7fr
5fr
3fr

12

CROSSROADS

WORDS & MUSIC BY ROBERT JOHNSON.
ARRANGED BY ERIC CLAPTON.

A
D
Down to the cross - road,
Down to the cross - road,
Go - in' down to Rose - dale,
Run, you can run;
A
fell down on my knees.
tried to flag a ride.
take my rid - er by my side.
tell my friend, Boy Wil - lie Brown
E
to Coda
Asked the Lord a - bove for mer - cy;
No - bo - dy seemed to know me,
We can still bar - rel - house ba - by,
that I'm stand - in' at the cross - road. Be -
D
A
1.2.
take me, if you please.
ev-ery-bo-dy passed me by.
on the riv - er - side.
I went down
Well, I'm
D.% al Coda
3.
CODA
D
A7
- lieve I'm sink - in' down.

COMIN' HOME

WORDS & MUSIC BY ERIC CLAPTON & BONNIE BRAMLETT.

14
GET READY

WORDS & MUSIC BY ERIC CLAPTON & YVONNE ELLIMAN.

you can't do those things that you're do-in' to me.
Rea-dy, get rea-dy, rea-dy,
he's a man who's gon-na break your heart.
Rea-dy, get
rea-dy, rea-dy, he's a man who's gon-na break your
heart.
I've ne-ver neeed-ed a run-nin' 'round diz-zy hound
check-in' out the bitch-es in heat,
You've got a lot-ta nerve, dish-ing out what you serve,

wag-gl-in' your piece of meat. Rea-dy, get rea-dy,
rea - dy, he's_ a man_____ who's gon-na break your
heart.
Rea-dy, get rea - dy, rea - dy,
he's_ a man_____ who's gon-na break your heart. I wan-na get_ re-venge
_ on your sin - ful sins, I got-ta get you back_____ for
what you did_ back then. And now you've got it back_
D.𝄋 and fade
life is mis-er - y,_ part_____ of you_ is a part of me.

GIVE ME STRENGTH

WORDS & MUSIC BY ERIC CLAPTON.

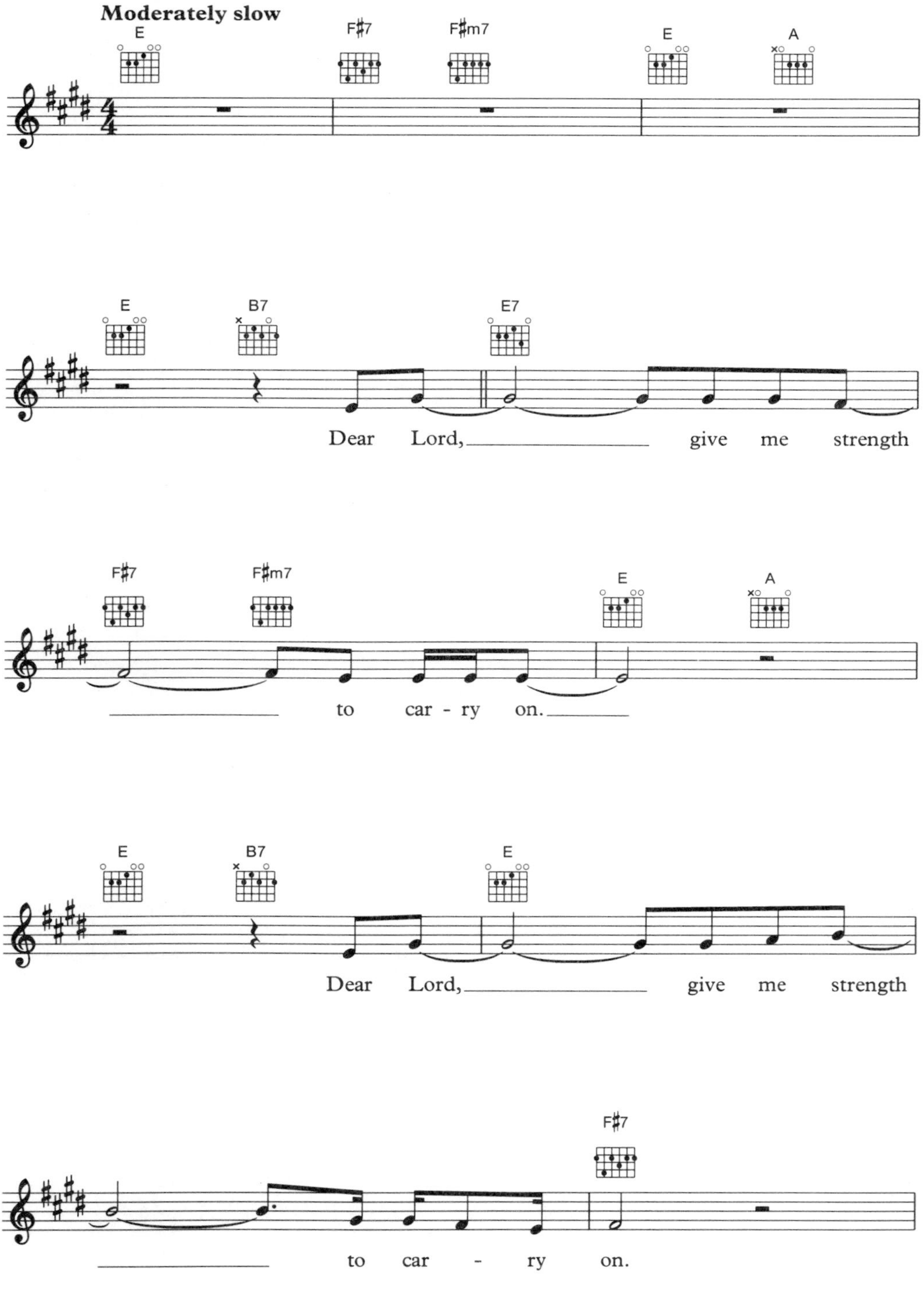

B7
E
My home may be out on the
E7
A
high - way, Lord, I've done so much wrong,
F♯7
F♯m7
E
so please, give me strength
F♯7
F♯m7
E
to car - ry on.
E7
A
Dear Lord, give me strength
B7
E7
A
D
to car - ry on.

A E7 A
Dear Lord give me
strength to car - ry on.
B7
E7 A
My home may be out on the
3
A7 D
high - way, Lord, I've done so much wrong,
B7 Bm7 A
but Lord, give me strength
B7 E7 D E
to car - ry on.

HAVE YOU EVER LOVED A WOMAN

WORDS & MUSIC BY BILLY MYLES.

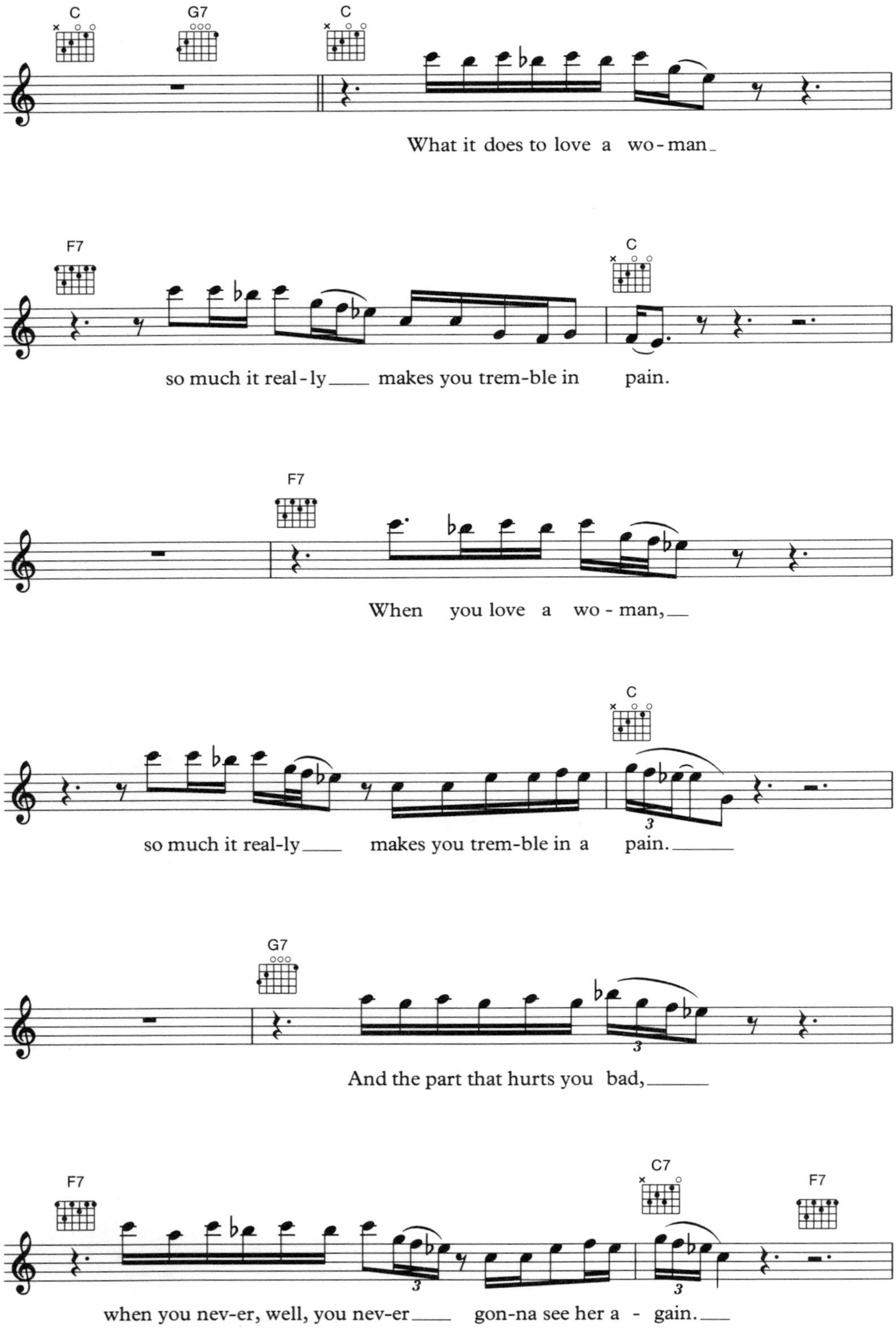
C
G7
C
What it does to love a wo-man
F7
C
so much it real-ly makes you trem-ble in pain.
F7
When you love a wo-man,
C
so much it real-ly makes you trem-ble in a pain.
G7
And the part that hurts you bad,
F7
C7
F7
when you nev-er, well, you nev-er gon-na see her a - gain.

C
G7
C7
Have you ev-er loved a wo-man
F7
C7
so much it real-ly, real-ly hurts to be a - lone?
Have you ev-er loved a wo-man
C
so much you real-ly, real-ly hate to be a - lone?
G7
Gb9
3fr
F9
All the time you know
she'll na-tur-al-ly break up your hap-py
C7
F7
C7
Db9
C9
home.
3

HELLO OLD FRIEND

WORDS & MUSIC BY ERIC CLAPTON.

G
D
I had to bend_ down
I got out_ and
but when he tipped his
C
G
just to have_ a peek._
walked to where you are._
hat I knew his name._
Hel-lo_ old friend,
Bm7
Am7
C
D
it's real-ly good to see_ you once a-gain.
Em
Bm7
Am7
Hel-lo old friend,_
it's real-ly good to see_
C
G
D
C
D
you once a-gain._

HOODOO MAN

WORDS & MUSIC BY AMOS 'JUNIOR' WELLS.

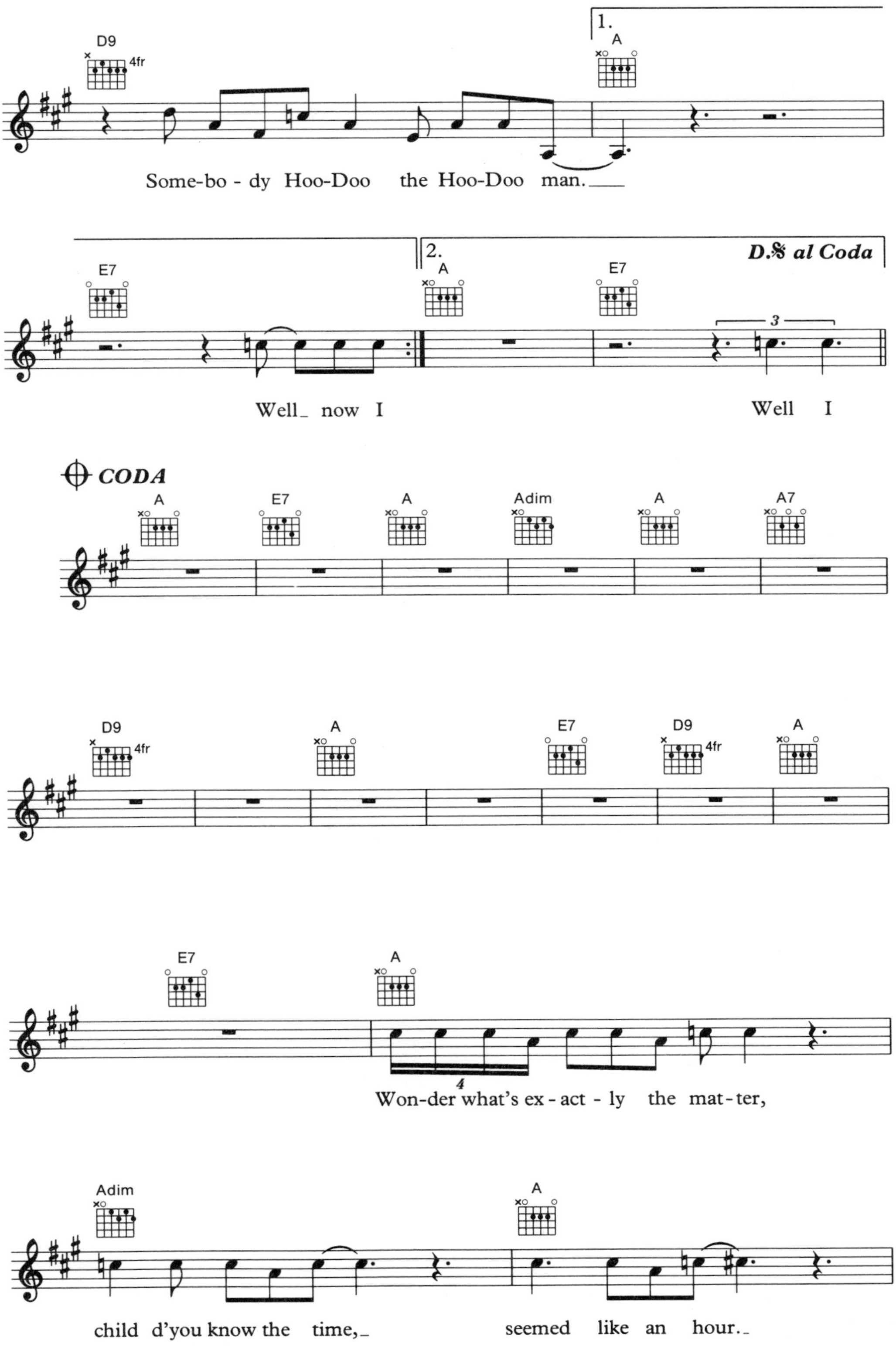
1.
D9
4fr
A
Some-bo - dy Hoo-Doo the Hoo-Doo man.
E7
2.
A
E7
D.𝄋 al Coda
3
Well now I
Well I
CODA
A
E7
A
Adim
A
A7
D9
4fr
A
E7
D9
4fr
A
E7
A
4
Won-der what's ex - act - ly the mat - ter,
Adim
A
child d'you know the time,
seemed like an hour.

2.3. Well now I buzzed your bell this morning
You had your elevator running slow
I buzzed your bell little woman
Well I hold up my head . . .

I CAN'T HOLD OUT

WORDS & MUSIC BY ELMORE JAMES.

know that I love you, I can't stand to see you cry, but I can't
A
E
hold out, I can't hold out too long,
B7
I get a real good feel - in'
A7
E
talk - in' to you on the phone." She said:
E
"Ba - by you can run, you can walk or fly, you
know that I love you, you're my heart's de - sire, I

A
E
can't hold out,
I can't hold out too long,
B7
A7
I get a real good feel-in'
talk-in' to you on the phone."
E
E
Talk to me ba - by,
A
talk to me ba - by,
talk to me ba - by,
E
B7
talk to me ba - by,
I get a real good feel - in'
A7
E
G9
A♭9
E7
9fr
10fr
12fr
talk-in' to you on the phone.

I CAN'T STAND IT

WORDS & MUSIC BY ERIC CLAPTON.

2.
Dm
Am
G
Dm
Am
G
Gm
3fr
Am
I can't stand it. You're
F
G
Am
F
G
Am
run-nin' a-round. I can't stand it. You're
F
G
Am
F
fool-in' a-round. I can't stand it. You're
G
Am
Dm
play-in' a-round with my heart. It was time,
Am
G
time for me to let you know.
Dm
Am
G
Ain't no crime, no crime to let your feel-ings show.

Am F
I can't stand__ it. You're
G Am F
run - nin' a - round, I can't stand__ it. You're
G Am F
play - in' a - round, I can't stand__ it. You're
G Am
fool - in' a - round,_ I can't stand__ it. You're
F G Am
run - nin' a - round, I can't stand__ it. You're
F G Am
play - in' a - round,_ I can't stand__ it.
F G Am
Fool - in' a - round,_ I can't stand__ it.

F G Am F G
Run-nin' a - round, I can't stand it. Run-nin' a - round, I won't
Am N.C. F G Am N.C.
stand it. Run-nin' a - round, I won't stand it. You're
F G Am N.C. F G
fool-in' a - round, I won't stand it. Play-in' a - round, I won't
Am N.C. F G Am
stand it. You're run-nin' a - round with my heart. You're
F G Am F G
fool-in' a - round with my heart,
Am F G Am F G
my heart. Run-nin' a - round with,
Am F G Am
repeat ad lib.
fool - in' a - round with my heart.

21

I FEEL FREE

WORDS & MUSIC BY JACK BRUCE & PETE BROWN.

hmm hmm hmm.
Hmm
hmm hmm hmm hm.
B D E
5fr 7fr
E D/E E D/E
7fr
Feel when I dance with you.
Dance floor is like the sea.
E D/E E D/E
7fr
We move like the sea.
Ceil - ing is the sky. You're the
E D/E E D
7fr 5fr
You, you're all I want to know.
sun, and as you shine on me,
E D
7fr 5fr
I feel free.

E
7fr
I feel free.
to Coda
E
7fr
I feel free. I can
E
7fr
walk down the street, there's no one there, though the
pave - ments are one huge crowd. I can
drive down the road, my eyes don't see, though my
mind wants to cry out loud.

E
D/E
E
D/E
Ah.
E
D/E
E
D/E
Ah.
E
D/E
E
Ah.
D
E
I feel free.
D
E
I feel free.
D
E
I feel free.
I can

C
walk down the street, there's no - one there, though the
B♭
A
pave-ments are one huge crowd. I can drive down the road, my eyes
F
won't see, though my mind wants to cry out loud.
D
D.𝄋 al Coda
though my mind wants to cry out loud.
CODA
E
7fr
D/E
7fr
free. Ah
3
repeat and fade
E
D/E
Ah.
3

IF I DON'T BE THERE BY MORNING

WORDS & MUSIC BY BOB DYLAN & HELENA SPRINGS.

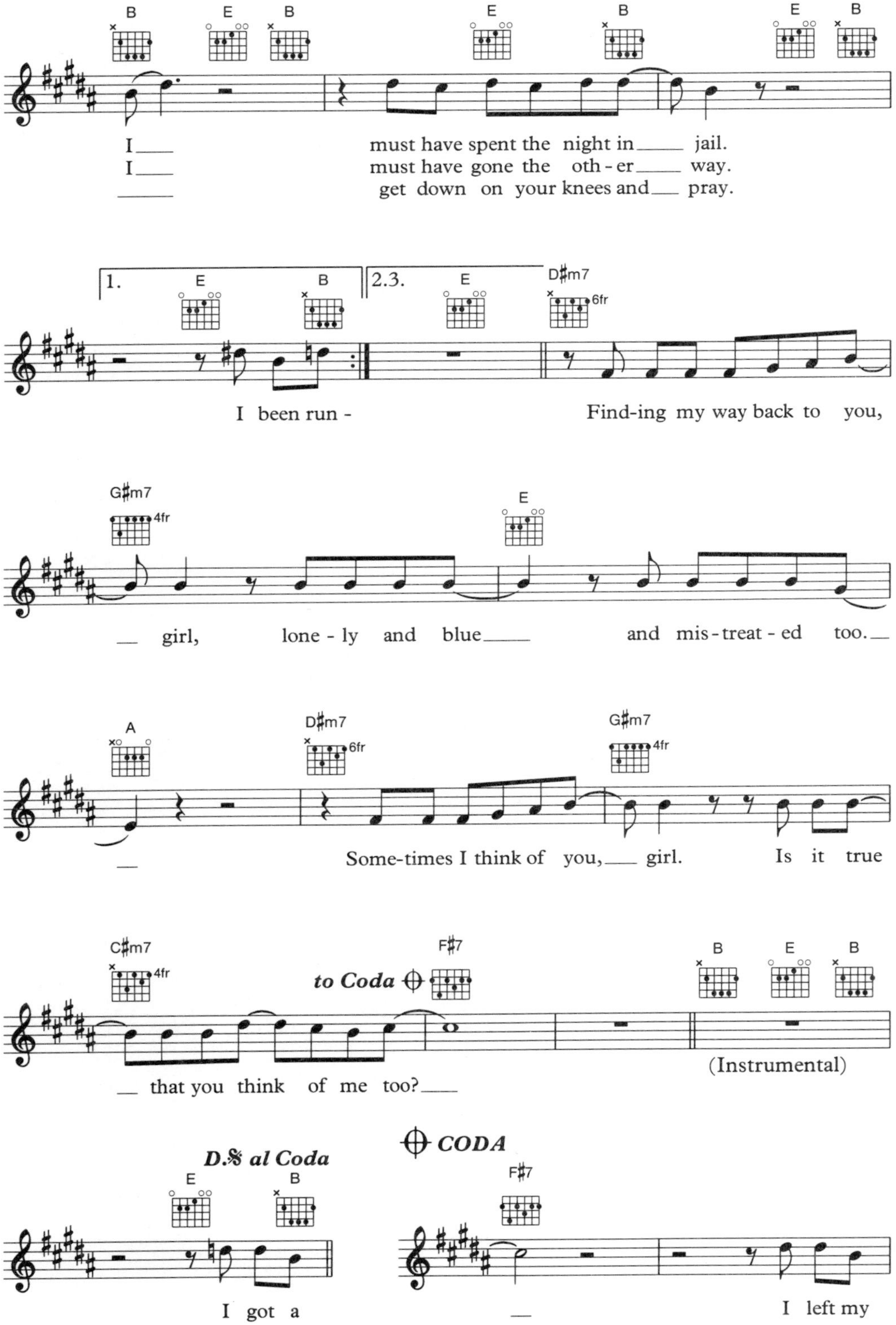
B E B E B E B
I___ must have spent the night in___ jail.
I___ must have gone the oth - er___ way.
___ get down on your knees and___ pray.
1. E B
I been run -
2.3. E
D♯m7 6fr
Find-ing my way back to you,
G♯m7 4fr E
___ girl, lone - ly and blue___ and mis - treat - ed too.___
A D♯m7 6fr G♯m7 4fr
___ Some-times I think of you,___ girl. Is it true
C♯m7 4fr
to Coda
F♯7
B E B
___ that you think of me too?___
(Instrumental)
D.𝄋 al Coda
E B
I got a
CODA
F♯7
___ I left my

B E B E B E B
wo-man with a twen-ty dol-lar bill.
E B E B E B
I left her wait-ing, I hope she's wait-ing for me_
E B E A/E E
_ still._ And if I_
A/E E A/E E A/E E
_ don't be there by morn-ing,_ I know that
B E B E B E B E B
I,_ I ne-ver will.
E B E B E B E B
Instrumental ad lib.

23

KEY TO THE HIGHWAY

WORDS & MUSIC BY BIG BILL BROONZY & CHAS. SEGAR.

E7 A A7 D/F♯ Dm/F
drove a good man _ a - way from home.
A E7 to Coda A E7
As the moon _ peeks o-ver the moun-tains,
D7 A
I'll be on _ my way. _ I'm gon-na roam _ this old high-way
E7 A A7 D/F♯ Dm/F A/E E7
un-til the break of day. _
A E7 D7 A E7 A A7 D/F♯ Dm/F
Instrumental ad lib.
A E7 D.𝄋 al Coda
I got the key
CODA
A7 E7 D7
A7 E7 A B♭7 A7 A9
4fr

KNOCKIN' ON HEAVEN'S DOOR

WORDS & MUSIC BY BOB DYLAN.

25

LAWDY MAMA

TRADITIONAL ARRANGED BY ERIC CLAPTON.

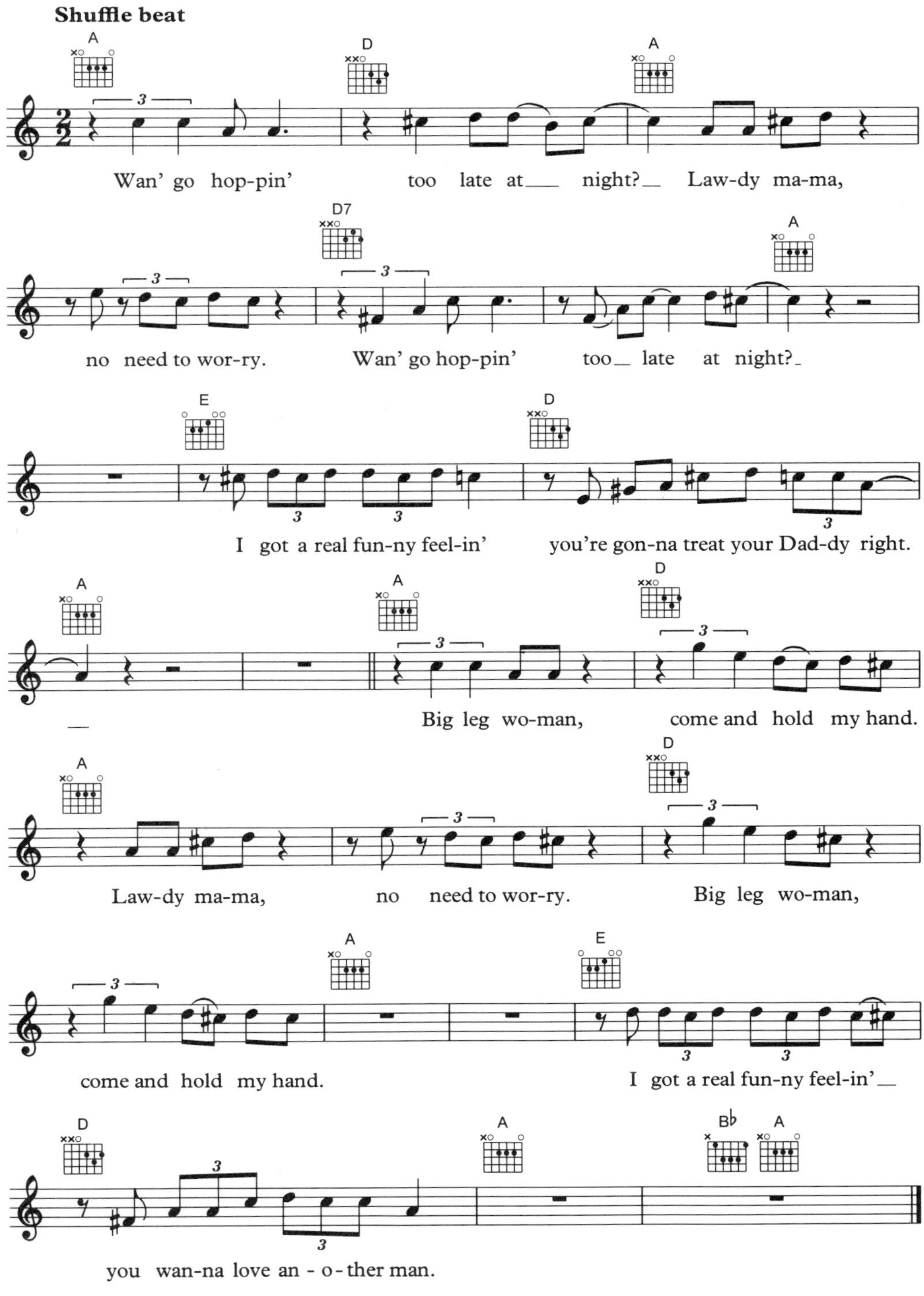

LAY DOWN SALLY

WORDS & MUSIC BY ERIC CLAPTON, MARCY LEVY & GEORGE TERRY.

D
Lay down Sal - ly, no need to leave so soon.
E
to Coda
1.
A
I've been try - ing all night long just to talk to you.
2. The
2.
A
D.C. al Coda
talk to you.
3. I
CODA
A
talk to you.
D
Lay down Sal - ly and rest here in my arms.
E
A
Don't you think you want some-one to talk to?
Lay down Sal -
D
E
- ly, no need to leave so soon.
I've been try - ing all
A
A
repeat and fade
night long just to talk to you.

27

LAYLA

WORDS & MUSIC BY ERIC CLAPTON & JIM GORDON.

B♭ C Dm B♭ C
- la, I'm beg-ging dar-lin' please. Lay - la
Dm B♭ C
dar-lin' won't you ease my wor-ried mind.
C♯m 4fr G♯m 4fr
Tried to give you con - so - la - tion,
Let's make the best of the sit - u - a - tion,
C♯m 4fr C D E
and your old man won't let you down.
be-fore I fin - 'lly go in - sane.
F♯m7 B E A
Like a fool I fell in love with you,
Please don't say that we'll ne-ver find a way,
F♯m7 B E Am
you turned the whole world up - side down. Lay -
and tell me all my love's in vain. Lay -

Dm
Bb
C
Dm
- la, you got me on my knees. Lay -
Bb
C
Dm
Bb
C
- la, I'm beg-ging dar-lin' please, Lay - la,
Dm
Bb
C
Dm
dar-lin' won't you ease my wor-ried mind. Lay -
Bb
C
Dm
- la, you've got me on my knees. Lay -
Bb
C
Dm
Bb
C
- la, I'm beg-ging dar-lin' please, Lay - la,
repeat ad lib. to fade
Dm
Bb
C
Dm
dar-lin' won't you ease my wor-ried mind.

LONELY STRANGER

C♯m7
4fr
E7
A
A♯dim7
but I don't know what's go -
E/B
C♯m7
4fr
F♯m7
B9
2nd time to Coda
- in' on,
so I'll be on my way.
E
A/E
Am6/E
E
A/E
Yes, I will.
Am6/E
E
A/E
Am6/E
E
Yes, I will.
Yes, I
D.C. al Coda
A/E
Am6/E
will.
CODA
E
A/E
Am6/E
E
A/E
Am6/E
E
Yes, I will.
Yes, I
A/E
Am6/E
E
A/E
will.
Yes, I will.

2. I was born with a raging thirst,
   A hunger to be free.
   But I've learned through the years,
   Don't encourage me.

3. When I walk, stay behind,
   Don't get close to me.
   'Cause it's sure to end in tears,
   So just let me be.

4. Some will say that I'm no good,
   Maybe I agree.
   Take a look, then walk away,
   That's alright with me.

LEAD ME ON

WORDS & MUSIC BY CECIL & LINDA WOMACK.

Bm G A/F♯ Bm G
Lead me on. Lead me on. Lead me on.
A/F♯ Bm Aadd9 Bm Aadd9 D6 D
I'll play a - long and a-long and a - long, Ba-by lead me
A E/G♯ 2fr A/F♯ A/E A E/G♯ 2fr A/F♯ A7 D A/C♯ Bm A
on. Lead me on.
1. D A/C♯ Bm E7
2. D A/C♯ Bm E7 A A/G
2. Pre-tend it's
D6/F♯ Ddim/F A A/G D6/F♯ Ddim/F
D.𝄋 al Coda
3. And when I
CODA
D A/C♯ Bm E7 A E/G♯ 2fr A/F♯ A/E
repeat ad lib. to fade
A E/G♯ 2fr A/F♯ A7 D A/C♯ Bm A D A/C♯ Bm E7
Lead me on. Lead me on.

LET IT GROW

WORDS & MUSIC BY ERIC CLAPTON.

D E G A
check out on my mind, try-ing hard to get a
much for you to do, on - ly ask and you_ will
Bm F♯7 D E
friend that I___ can count on, but there's no - thing left__ to show,
get what you are need - ing, the rest is up__ to you,
G A B B
plant your love and let it grow.
plant your love and let it grow.
Let it grow, let it
E B A B
grow, let it blos-som let_ it flow. In the sun, the rain, the
E B A 1. F♯7
snow, love is love-ly,___ let_ it grow.
2. F♯7
grow.
repeat and fade
Bm F♯7 D E G A

31

MAINLINE FLORIDA

WORDS & MUSIC BY GEORGE TERRY.

E
Her arms were o - pen, o-pen wide, her in - vi - ta - tion's a
chang - ing tide._ I could re-mem - ber not long a - go,
we took a cruise down on ho - tel row.________ Main-line
A
D
E
A
E
A
D
Flo - ri - da,_ oh___ say,________ Main-line Flo - ri - da,_ o -
G
F♯
F
N.C.
repeat and fade
- kay.__________

MEAN OLD FRISCO

WORDS & MUSIC BY ARTHUR CRUDUP.

E
A
E
B7
A
E
D.𝄋 al Coda
4. Well, that
CODA
E
A
E
A
E
me.
(hum)
A
E
B7
A
E
E/G♯
2fr
A
A♯dim7
B7
E

33
MOTHERLESS CHILDREN

TRADITIONAL.
ARRANGED BY ERIC CLAPTON & CARL RADLE.

D
A
D
mo-ther will when your mo-ther is dead, Lord.
A
D
1. Fa-ther will do the best he can when your mo-
2. Sis-ter will do the best she can when your mo-
A
D
A
-ther is dead, Lord. Fa-ther will do the
-ther is dead, Lord. Sis-ter will do the
D
A
D
best he can when your mo-ther is dead, Lord.
best she can when your mo-ther is dead, Lord.
A
E
D
Fa-ther will do the best he can, so ma-ny things a fa-ther
Sis-ter will do the best she can, so ma-ny things a sis-ter
F
A
can't un-der-stand. No-bo-dy treats you like a mo-
can't un-der-stand. No-bo-dy treats you like a mo-

D
A
1.
D
- ther will__ when your mo - ther is dead, Lord.
- ther will__ when your mo - ther is dead, Lord.
(Instrumental)
2.
D
A
D
When your mo - ther is dead,___ when your mo -
A
D
A
- ther is dead. When your mo - ther is dead, Lord,
D
A
D
A
when your mo - ther is dead.__
Instrumental
E
D
F
A
D
A
D

PLEASE BE WITH ME

WORDS & MUSIC BY CHARLES SCOTT BOYER.

Moderate Country style

G D A
— it was I'd said___ that made me think___ I'd lost my
Bm G
head when I____ knew I'd lost my heart in -
D C
- stead.________________ So won't you
G D Em D
please read my_ signs? Be a gyp - sy. Tell me_
G D Em
what I hope to find____ deep with - in_____ me,
D G D
be-cause you can find_ my_ mind, please be with_

Bm
D
G
to Coda
me.
D
G
D
Of all the bet-ter things I've heard, lov-in' you
G
D
A
has made the words and all the rest seem so ab - surd,
Bm
G
'cause in the end it all comes out, I'm
D
C
D.S. al Coda
sure.
Won't you
CODA
D
G
D
G
D
G
D

35

NO ALIBIS

D A/D G/D A/D D A/D G/D A/D
D A/D G/D D A/D G/D
A Bm G D
1. I beg your par - don, hel - lo darl - in',
2. And it gets steep-er, the hole you dig gets deep-er,
3. Moun-tain gets steep-er, the hole you dig is get-ting deep-er,
G D A
this is me you're talk - in' to,
you better stop and climb out,
you better reach and pull your-self out,
Bm G D
sit down and tell me a-bout it, you don't have to shout it at me,
try - ing to give it all to you, ba - by, I can see right through you,
no-one's ev - er gon-na love you, the way that I love you,
G D A D
tell me what you real-ly want to do. Don't give me no
some-times you lose what it's all about.
I ne - ver wan-na to see you doin' without.

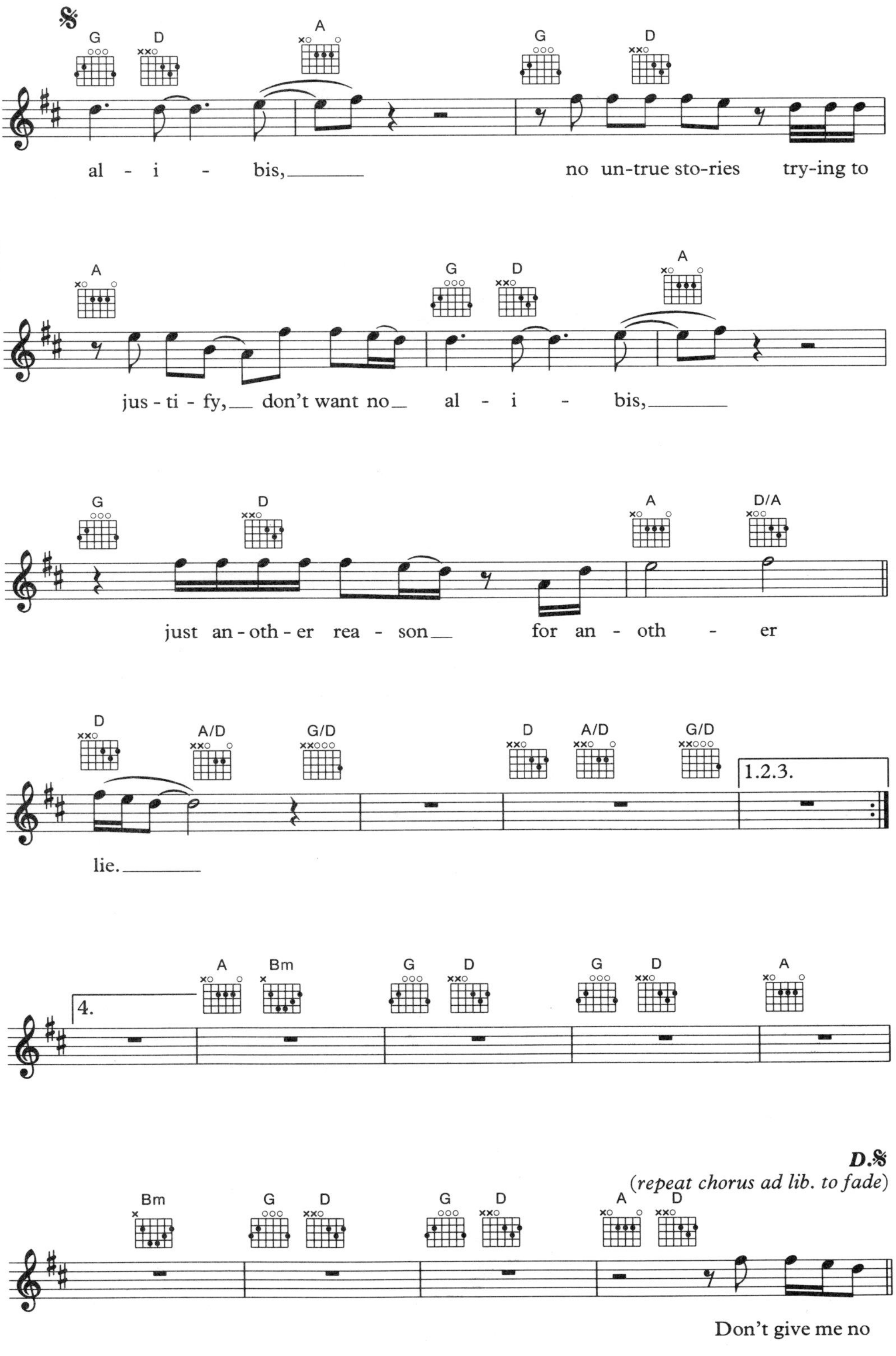
G D A G D
al - i - bis, no un-true sto-ries try-ing to
A G D A
jus - ti - fy, don't want no al - i - bis,
G D A D/A
just an-oth-er rea - son for an - oth - er
D A/D G/D D A/D G/D
1.2.3.
lie.
4.
A Bm G D G D A
D.𝄋
(repeat chorus ad lib. to fade)
Bm G D G D A D
Don't give me no

NOBODY KNOWS YOU WHEN YOU'RE DOWN AND OUT

WORDS & MUSIC BY JIMMIE COX.

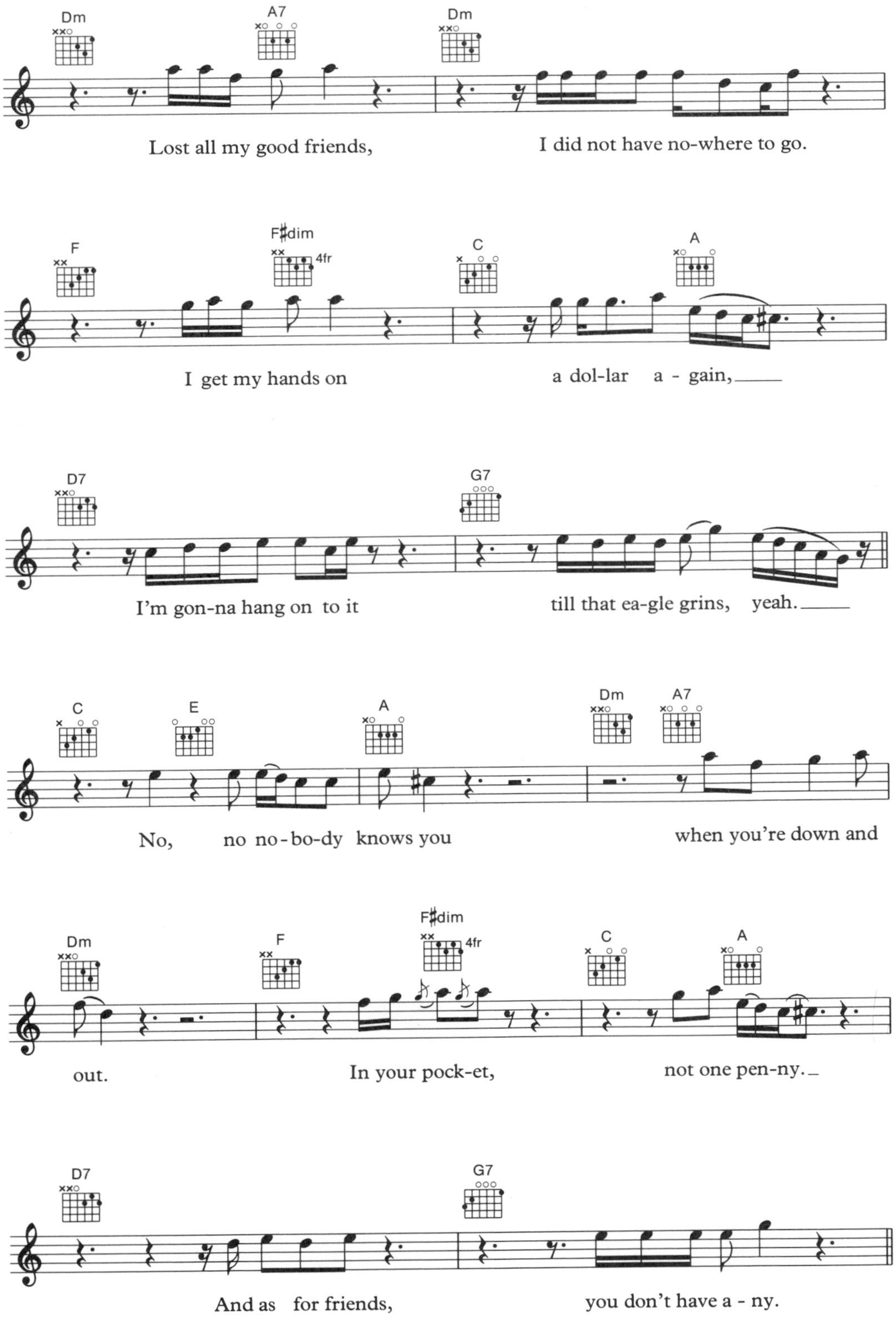
Dm
A7
Dm
Lost all my good friends,
I did not have no-where to go.
F
F♯dim
4fr
C
A
I get my hands on
a dol-lar a - gain,
D7
G7
I'm gon-na hang on to it
till that ea-gle grins, yeah.
C
E
A
Dm
A7
No, no no-bo-dy knows you
when you're down and
Dm
F
F♯dim
4fr
C
A
out.
In your pock-et,
not one pen-ny.
D7
G7
And as for friends,
you don't have a - ny.

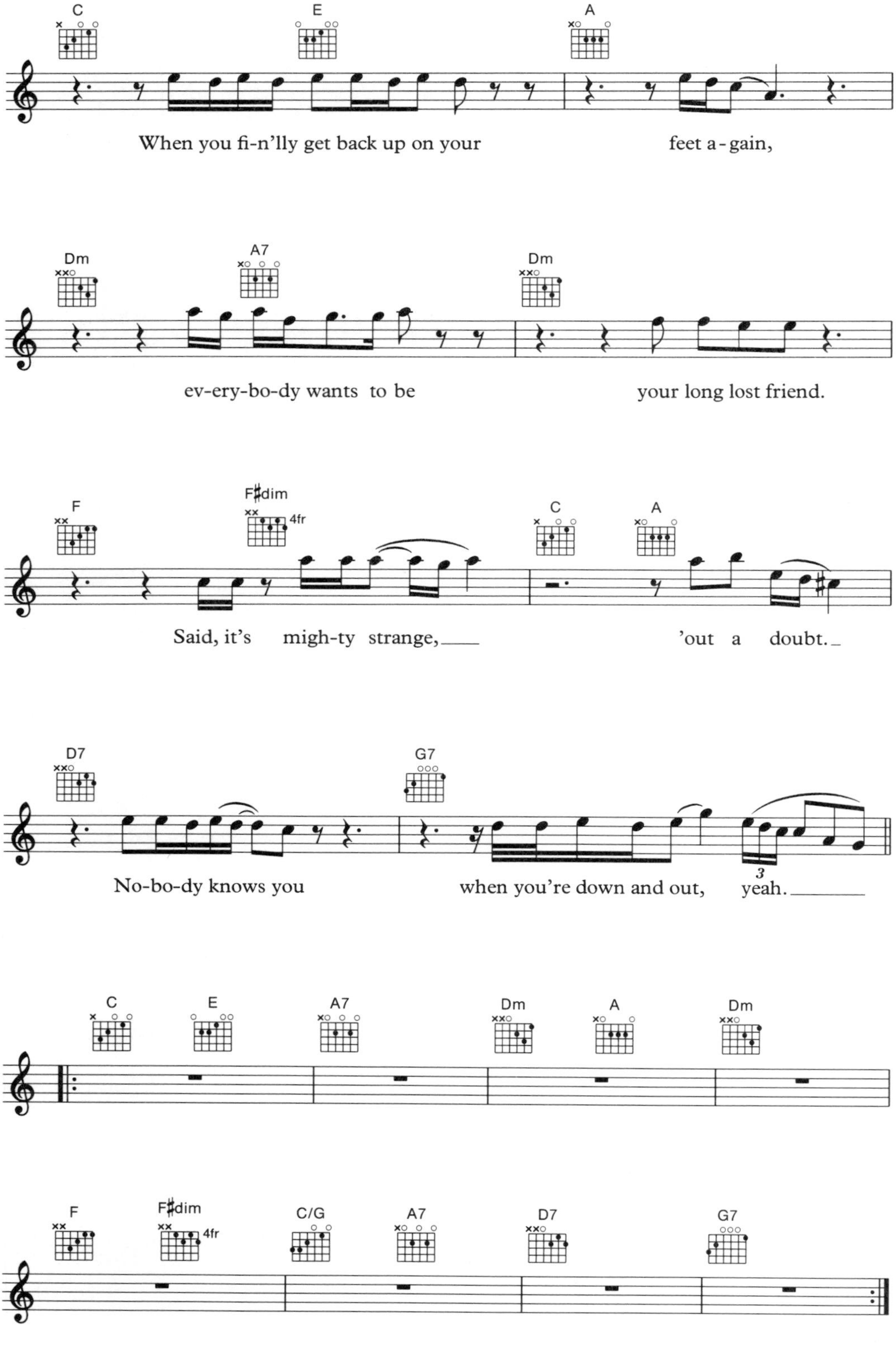
C E A
When you fi-n'lly get back up on your feet a-gain,
Dm A7 Dm
ev-ery-bo-dy wants to be your long lost friend.
F F♯dim 4fr C A
Said, it's migh-ty strange, 'out a doubt.
D7 G7
No-bo-dy knows you when you're down and out, yeah.
3
C E A7 Dm A Dm
F F♯dim 4fr C/G A7 D7 G7

C E A
And when you fi-n'lly get back up on your feet a-gain,
Dm A7 Dm
ev-ery-bo-dy wants to be your good old long lost friend.
F F♯dim 4fr C A
Said, it's migh-ty strange, yeah.
D7 E♭7 E7
No - bo - dy knows you,
F7 3fr E♭7 E7 D7
no-bo - dy knows, no-bo - dy knows you
G7 C C7 8fr
when you're down and out.

37
OLD LOVE

WORDS & MUSIC BY ERIC CLAPTON & ROBERT CRAY.

E7 F F7 E7
When will I ev-er learn? Old
Am F/D Gsus4 G Am F/D Gsus4 G
love leave me a-lone.
Am F/D Gsus4 G Am F/D 1. Gsus4 G
Old love go on home.
2. Gsus4 G Am F/D Gsus4 G Am F Gsus4 G
F E7 Am G♯aug5 C/G Am/F♯ F E7
F F7 E7 Am F/D Gsus4 G
Old love leave
Am F/D Gsus4 G Am F/D Gsus4 G
me a-lone. Old love
to fade
Am F/D Gsus4 G Am F/D Gsus4 G Am F/D Gsus4 G
go on home. Instrumental

ONE MORE CHANCE

WORDS & MUSIC BY ERIC CLAPTON.

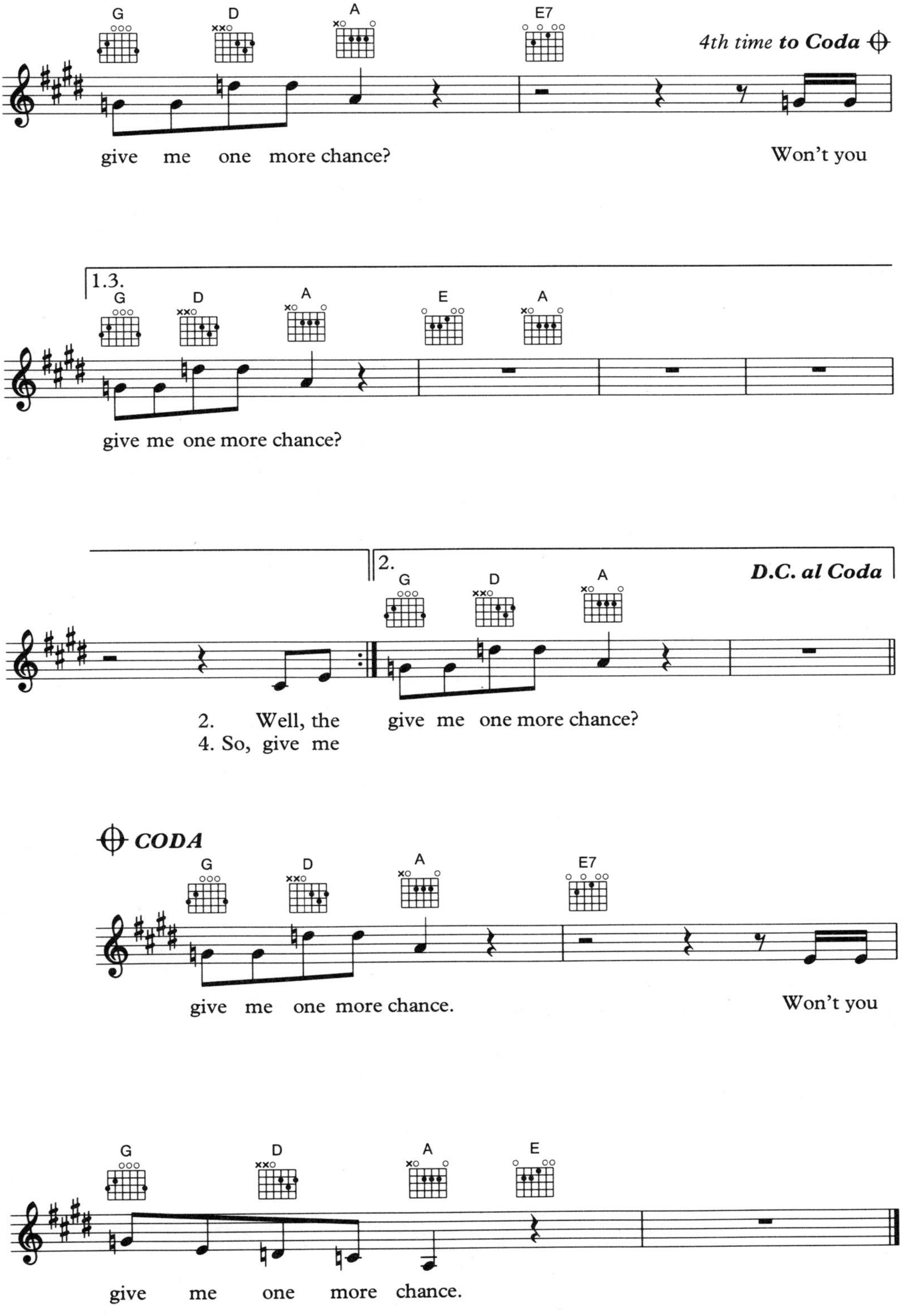
G D A E7
4th time to Coda
give me one more chance?
Won't you
1.3.
G D A E A
give me one more chance?
2.
D.C. al Coda
G D A
2. Well, the
4. So, give me
give me one more chance?
CODA
G D A E7
give me one more chance.
Won't you
G D A E
give me one more chance.

39

PRESENCE OF THE LORD

WORDS & MUSIC BY ERIC CLAPTON.

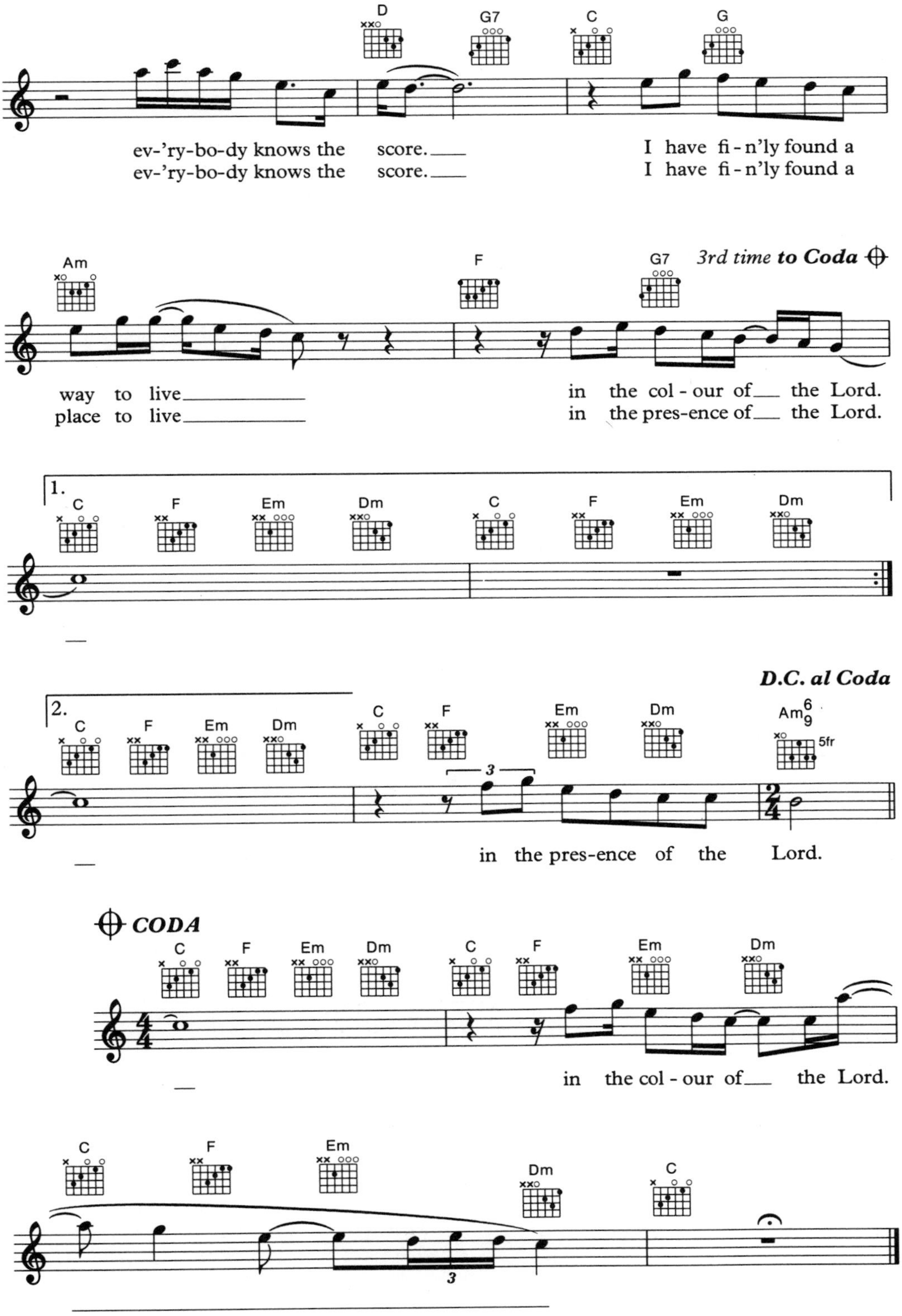
D G7 C G
ev-'ry-bo-dy knows the score.__ I have fi-n'ly found a
ev-'ry-bo-dy knows the score.__ I have fi-n'ly found a
Am F G7
3rd time to Coda
way to live__ in the col-our of__ the Lord.
place to live__ in the pres-ence of__ the Lord.
1.
C F Em Dm C F Em Dm
D.C. al Coda
2.
C F Em Dm C F Em Dm Am6/9
5fr
in the pres-ence of the Lord.
CODA
C F Em Dm C F Em Dm
in the col-our of__ the Lord.
C F Em Dm C

PRETENDING

WORDS & MUSIC BY JERRY LYNN WILLIAMS.

E5
3rd time to Coda
A
E
__ night. __
__ strange. __
That's when she said she was pre -
D
A
E
D
- tend - ing, _
like she knew the plan, __
A
E
D
that's when I knew she was pre - tend - ing, _
pre -
A
E
D
E5
- tend-ing to un - der - stand. __
Pre - tend - ing.
G/E
D/E
Pre - tend - ing. _
Pre -
A
E5
- tend - ing. _
Pre - tend - ing. _
1.
2.
E5
G/E
Instrumental

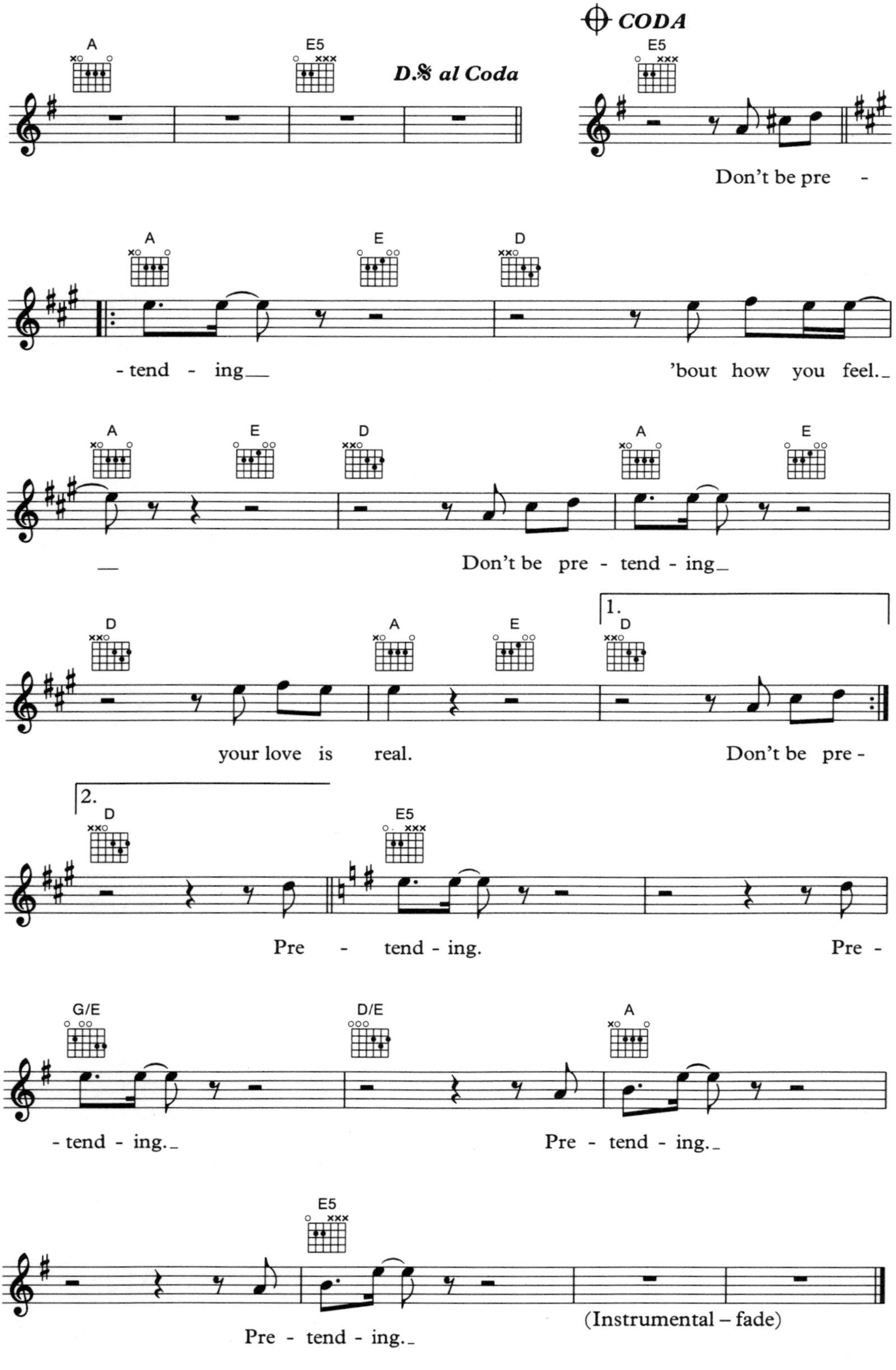
A
E5
D.𝄋 al Coda
⊕ CODA
E5
Don't be pre -
A
E
D
- tend - ing
'bout how you feel.
A
E
D
A
E
Don't be pre - tend - ing
D
A
E
1.
D
your love is real.
Don't be pre -
2.
D
E5
Pre - tend - ing.
Pre -
G/E
D/E
A
- tend - ing.
Pre - tend - ing.
E5
Pre - tend - ing.
(Instrumental – fade)

41
ROLL IT OVER

WORDS & MUSIC BY ERIC CLAPTON & BOBBY WHITLOCK.

C♯m
4fr
F♯7
G♯7
4fr
much it means_ to be here in your arms._
C♯m
4fr
C♯m/B
A7
Roll it o -
E
- ver. Roll it o - ver.
E
Go down ea - sy and let me take my time.___
Roll it o - ver, let's take it from be - hind.___
A7
Go down ea -
Roll it o -
- sy and let me take my time.___
- ver, let's take it from be - hind.___

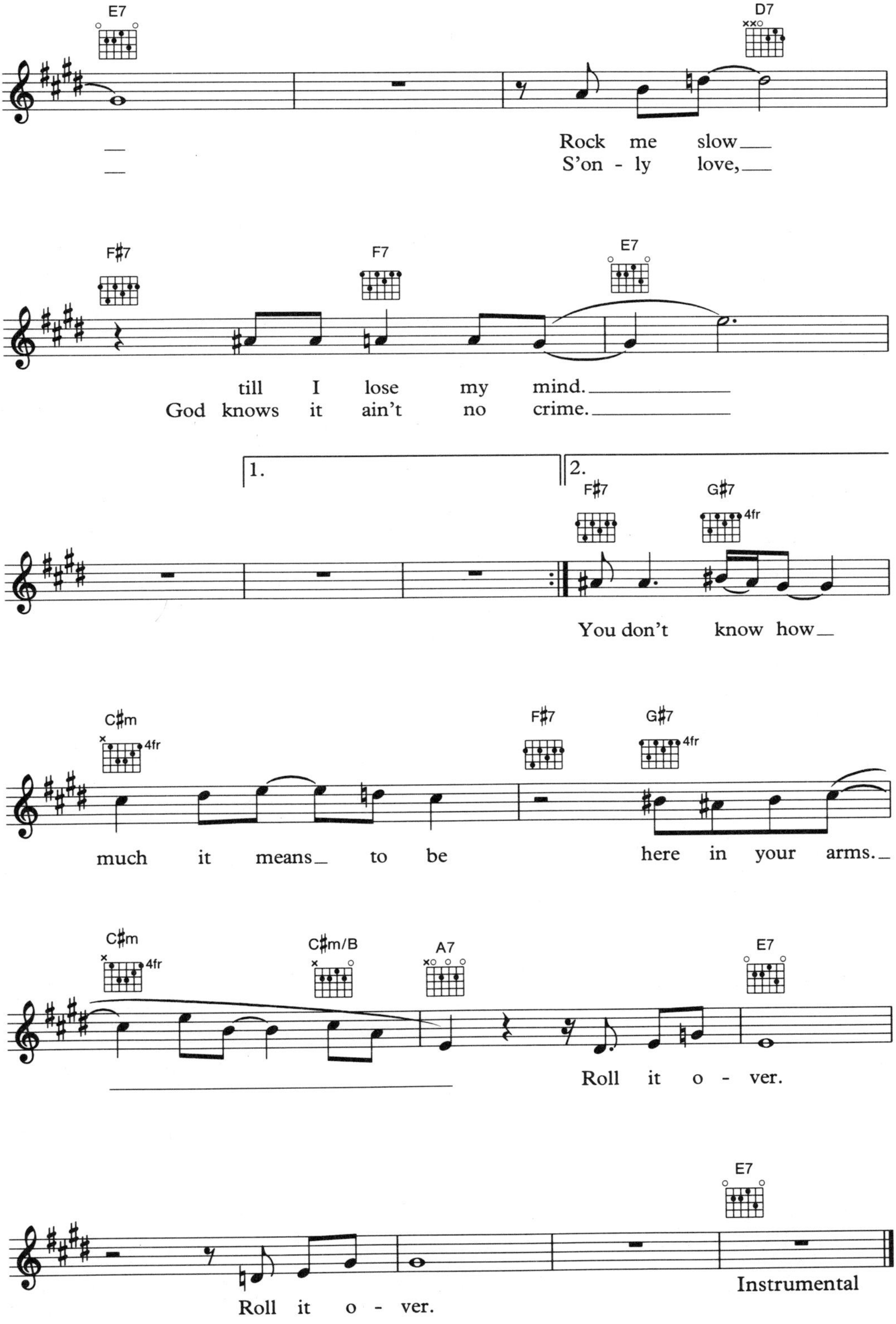
E7
D7
Rock me slow
S'on - ly love,
F♯7
F7
E7
till I lose my mind.
God knows it ain't no crime.
1.
2.
F♯7
G♯7
4fr
You don't know how
C♯m
4fr
F♯7
G♯7
4fr
much it means to be here in your arms.
C♯m
4fr
C♯m/B
A7
E7
Roll it o - ver.
E7
Roll it o - ver.
Instrumental

RAMBLIN' ON MY MIND

WORDS & MUSIC BY ROBERT JOHNSON.
ARRANGED BY ERIC CLAPTON.

2.
B7
A7
blues 'bout Miss So and So,
and the sun got the blues 'bout me.
E
B7
E
3. I got
E
A7
mean things,
I've got mean things all on my mind,
E
A
lit - tle girl, lit-tle girl,
E
I've got mean things all on my mind.
B7
Is to leave my ba - by,
A7
E
D♯7
E7
'cause she treat me so un - kind.

43

ROLLIN' AND TUMBLIN'

WORDS & MUSIC BY MUDDY WATERS.

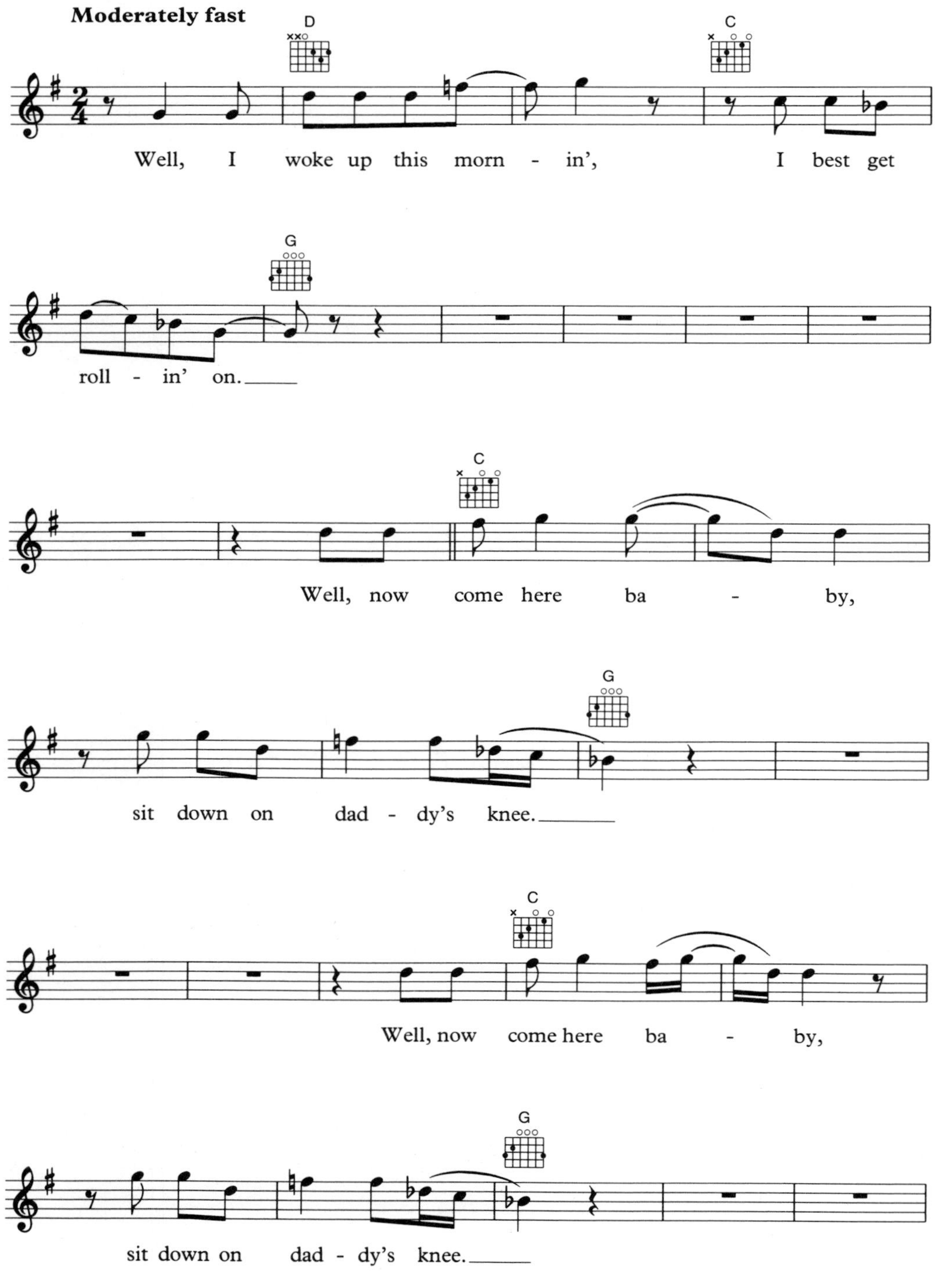

D
I wan - na tell you a - bout the
C
G
way they treat - ed me.
C
Well, I rolled and I tumb - led, cried the
G
whole night long.
C
Well, I rolled and I tumb - led, cried the
G
whole night long.
When I
D
G
woke up this morn - in', all I had was gone.

RUNNING ON FAITH

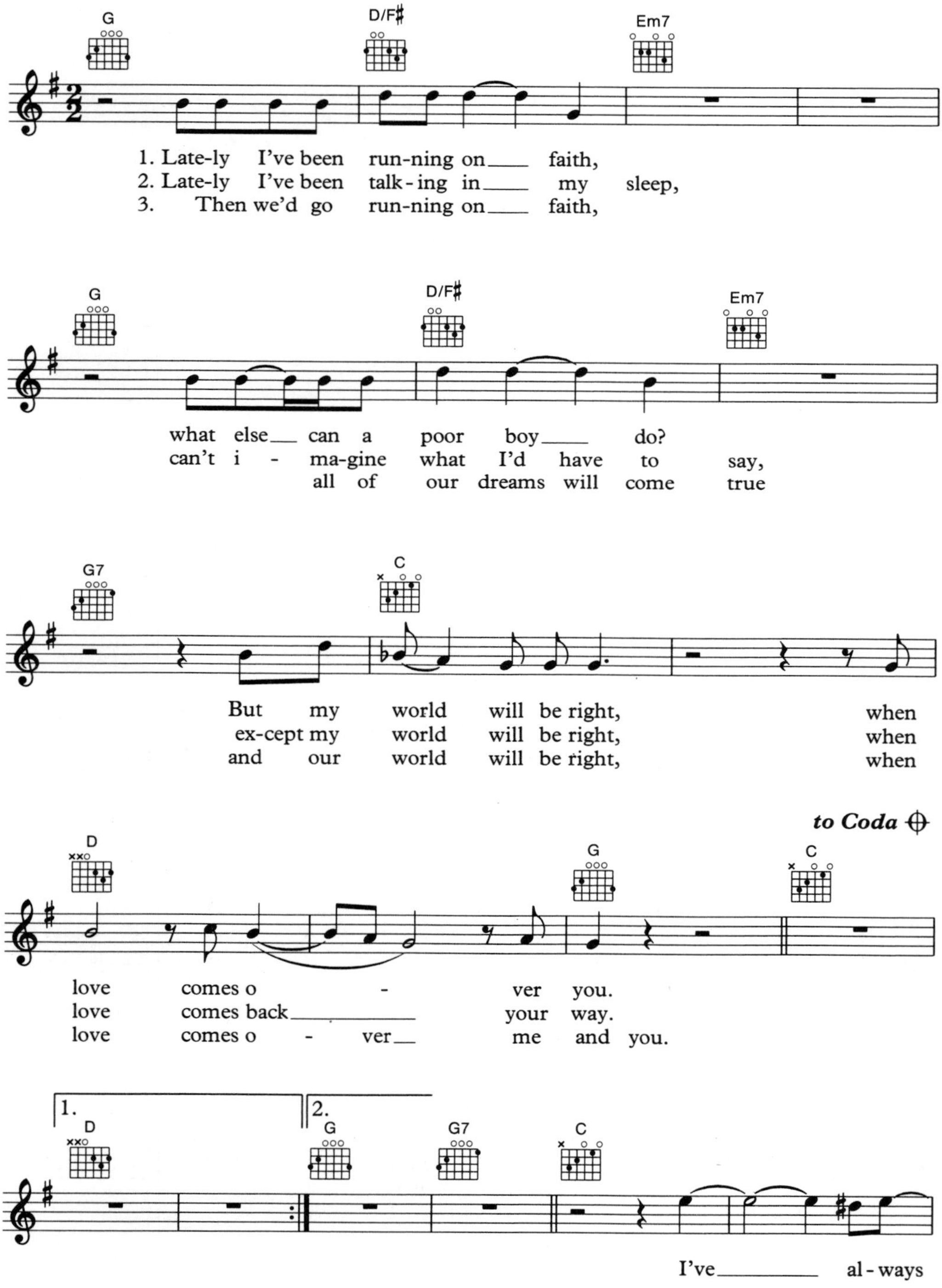

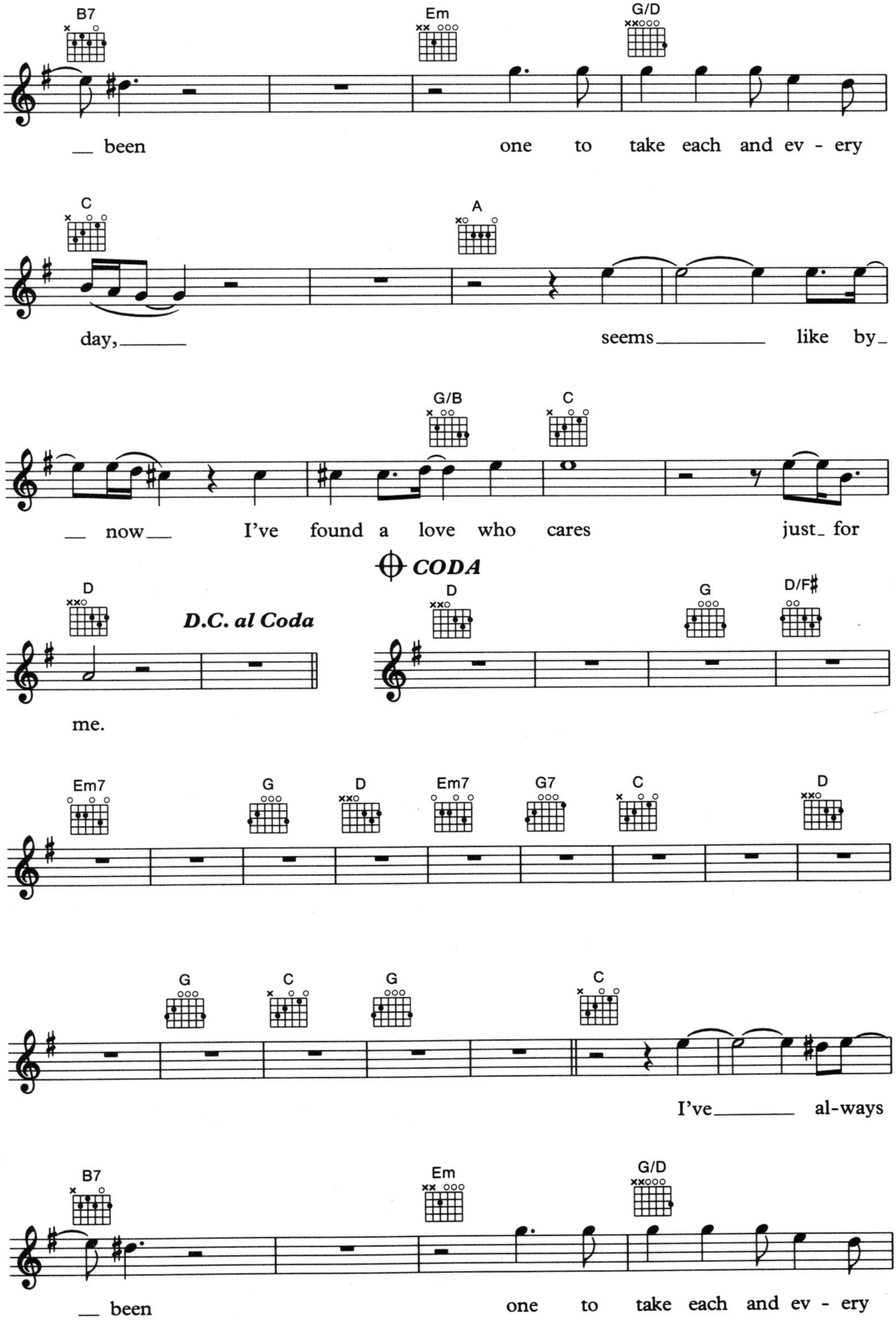
B7 Em G/D
been one to take each and ev - ery
C A
day, seems like by
now
G/B C
I've found a love who cares just for
D
D.C. al Coda
me.
CODA
D G D/F♯
Em7 G D Em7 G7 C D
G C G C
I've al-ways
B7 Em G/D
been one to take each and ev - ery

C
A
day, seems like by
G/B
C
now I've found a love who cares just for
D
G
D/F♯
me. 4. Then we'd go run-ning on faith,
G
D/F♯
all of our dreams will come true
Em7
G7
C
all the world will be right, when
D
F
C
F
love comes o - ver you. When
G
F
C
repeat ad lib.
love comes o - ver you. When

45
TALES OF BRAVE ULYSSES

WORDS & MUSIC BY ERIC CLAPTON & MARTIN SHARP.

D F G B♭
spark-ling waves are call - ing you to kiss their white laced lips.
carv - ing deep blue rip - ples in the tis - sues of your mind.
1.
A7 D C A D C
And you
2.
A D C A D C
D
Ti - ny pur - ple fish - es run laugh-ing through your fin - gers, and you
want to take her with you to the hard land__ of the win-ter.
D C G/B B♭ D C G/B B♭
Her
D C G/B B♭
name is Aph - ro - di - te and she rides a crim-son shell._ And you

D F G B♭
know you can - not leave her, for you touched the dis - tant sands_ with
D F G B♭
tales of brave U - lys - ses; how his na - ked ears were tor-tured by the
D C D C
si - rens sweet - ly sing - in'.
G/B B♭ D C G/B B♭
And the
D
ti - ny pur - ple fish - es run laugh-ing through your fin - gers, and you
want to take her with you_ to the hard land_ of the win - ter._
D C G/B B♭ D C G/B B♭

SPOONFUL

WORDS & MUSIC BY WILLIE DIXON.

spoon - ful. That spoon, that spoon, that spoon.
Could fill a spoons-ful of cof - fee; Could fill a spoons-ful of tea.
Just a lit-tle spoon of your pre-cious love, is
that e - nough for me? Men lies a-bout it.
Some of them cries a-bout it. Some of them
dies a-bout it. Ev - 'ry-thing's a fight-in' a-bout the
spoon - ful. That spoon, that spoon, that spoon - ful. That
spoon, that spoon, that spoon - ful. That spoon, that spoon, that

spoon - ful.__ That spoon, that spoon, hey.________
Could fill a spoons-ful of wa - ter,__ saved them from the des-ert sands.
____ Was a lit - tle spoon of your love, ba - by,____
saved you from an-o-ther man. Men lies________ a some of them
__ cries________ a - bout it.__ Some of them dies.______________
Ev-'ry-thing's a - fight-in' a-bout it. uh__ Ev-'ry-thing's a -
- cry-in' a-bout it.__________ uh Ev-'ry-thing's a, ev-'ry-thing's a -
- dy-in' a-bout it. Ev-'ry-thing's a - cry-in' a-bout it. Ev-'ry-thing's a -

- ly-in' a-bout it.
Lit'l' old, lit'l' old,
spoon - ful,
spoon - ful,
Hey!
Ev - 'ry - thing's dy-in' a-bout it, yh.
Al-right, just
cry-in' a-bout it.
That spoon, that spoon, that
lit-tle old spoon, lit-tle old spoon, lit-tle old lit-tle old
spoon, lit-tle old spoon, lit-tle old spoon - ful. That spoon, that spoon, that
spoon - ful. Spoon, that spoon, that spoon - ful. Yeah.
Freely
G
E7♯9
Ev - 'ry-thing's a - dy-in' a-bout it.
Hey!

47

STEADY ROLLIN' MAN

WORDS & MUSIC BY ROBERT JOHNSON.
ARRANGED BY ERIC CLAPTON.

A
man that rolls__ when i - ci - cles_ are hang-in' on the trees,
D C
I am a man that rolls____
D C A
when i - ci - cles are hang-in' on the trees,
E
but can't you hear me beg - gin', ma - ma,__
D G A♭ 3fr 4fr A 5fr
D.𝄋 al Coda
ooh Lord, down on my bend-ed knee.__ I am a
CODA
A 5fr A 5fr
repeat and fade

STRANGE BREW

WORDS & MUSIC BY ERIC CLAPTON, MIKE COLLINS & FELIX PAPPALARDI.

A
5fr
E7#9
6fr
D7#9
4fr
Strange brew, kill-in' what's in-side_ of you.
A
5fr
On a boat in the mid-dle of the
D9
4fr
A
5fr
D9
4fr
rag-ing_ sea, she would make a scene for it all to be ig-nored,
A
5fr
E7#9
6fr
and would-n't you be bored._ Strange brew,
D7#9
4fr
A
5fr
D9
4fr
kill-in' what's in-side_ of you. Strange brew,
A
5fr
D7#9
4fr
A
5fr
strange brew, strange brew, strange__ brew,
E7#9
6fr
D7#9
4fr
A
5fr
Am9
strange brew, kill-in' what's in-side_ of you.

SUNSHINE OF YOUR LOVE

WORDS & MUSIC BY JACK BRUCE, PETE BROWN & ERIC CLAPTON.

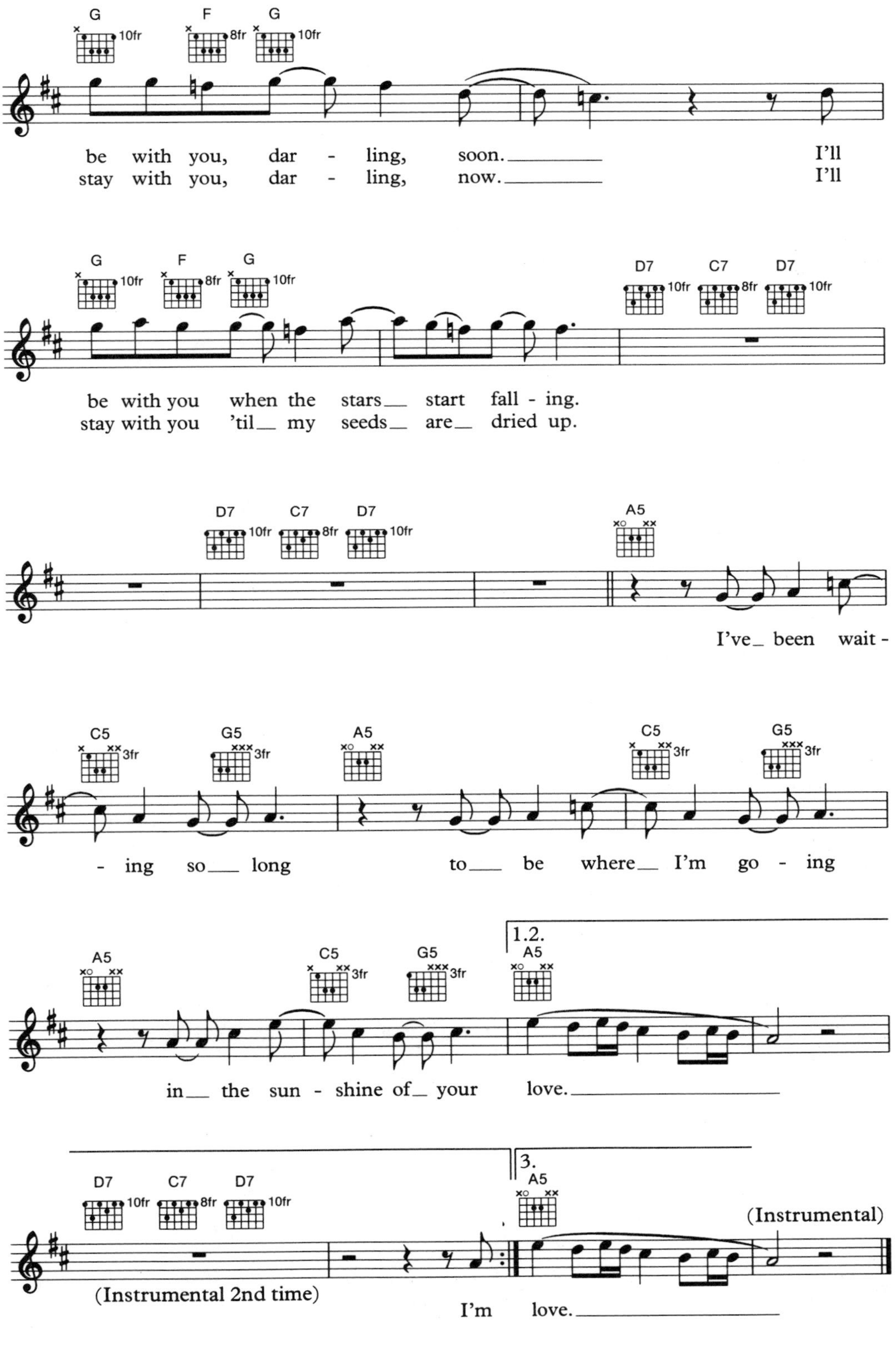
G F G
be with you, dar - ling, soon.
stay with you, dar - ling, now.
I'll
I'll
G F G D7 C7 D7
be with you when the stars start fall - ing.
stay with you 'til my seeds are dried up.
D7 C7 D7 A5
I've been wait -
C5 G5 A5 C5 G5
- ing so long to be where I'm go - ing
A5 C5 G5
1.2.
A5
in the sun - shine of your love.
D7 C7 D7
(Instrumental 2nd time)
3.
A5
(Instrumental)
I'm love.
10fr
8fr
3fr

TEARS IN HEAVEN

WORDS & MUSIC BY ERIC CLAPTON & WILL JENNINGS.

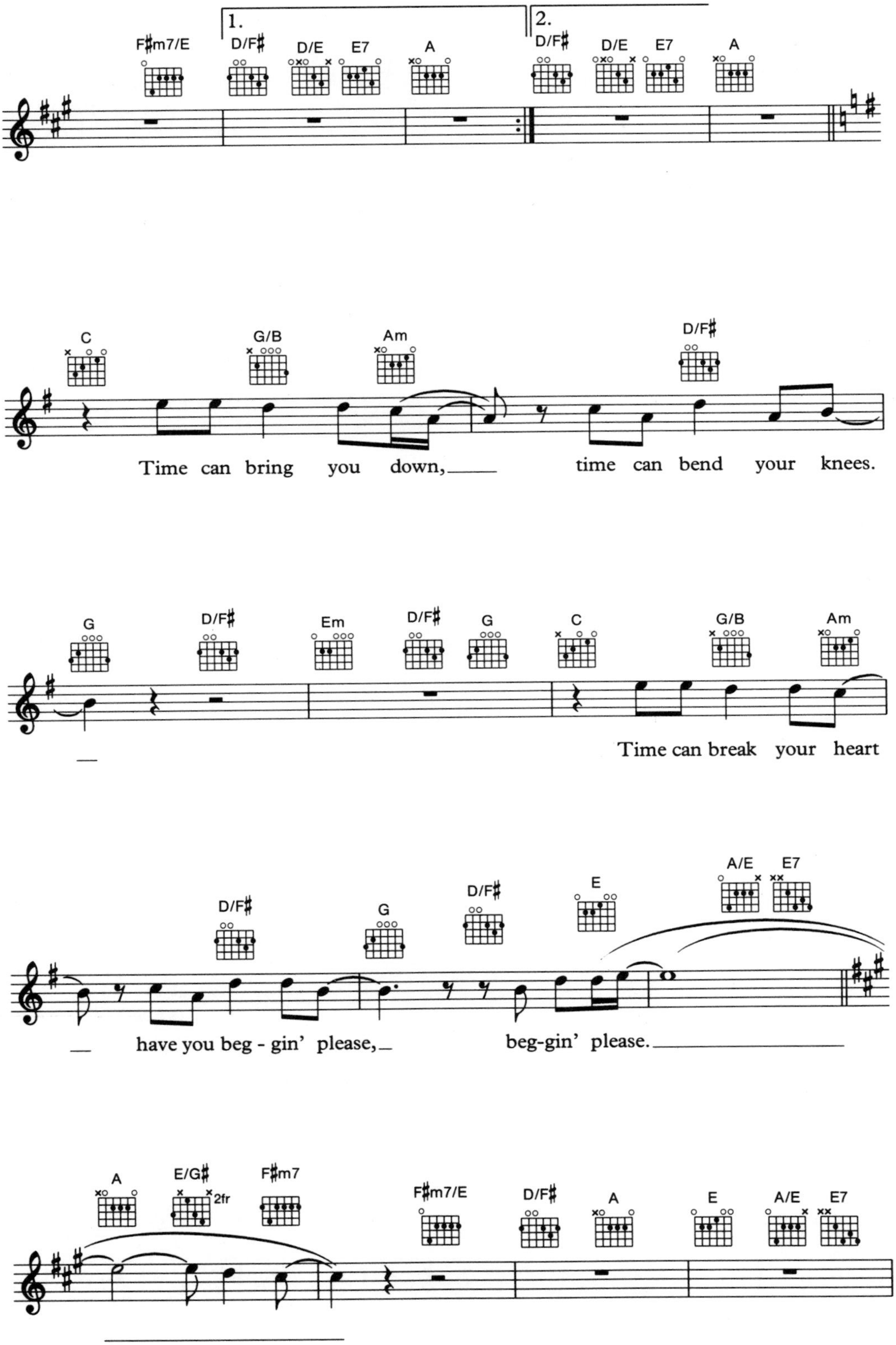

1.
2.
F♯m7/E D/F♯ D/E E7 A D/F♯ D/E E7 A
C G/B Am D/F♯
Time can bring you down, time can bend your knees.
G D/F♯ Em D/F♯ G C G/B Am
Time can break your heart
D/F♯ G D/F♯ E A/E E7
have you beg - gin' please, beg-gin' please.
A E/G♯ 2fr F♯m7 F♯m7/E D/F♯ A E A/E E7

A E/G♯ F♯m7 F♯m7/E D/F♯ A E A/E E7
F♯m C♯/E♯ A7/E
Be-yond the door there's peace, I'm sure,
F♯7 G♯m F♯/A♯ Bm7 D/E
and I know there'll be no more tears in hea -
D.C. al Coda
A E/G♯ F♯m7 F♯m7/E D/F♯ D/E E7 A
- ven.
CODA
A E/G♯ F♯m7 F♯m7/E Bm7
- ven. 'cause I know I don't be-long
D/E A E/G♯ F♯m F♯m7/E D/F♯ D/E E7 A
here in hea - ven.

TELL THE TRUTH

WORDS & MUSIC BY ERIC CLAPTON & BOBBY WHITLOCK.

G
D
the whole world is shak - in' now. Can't you feel
E
B E B E B E
G
it?
A new dawn is break -
D
1.
B7
- in' now. Can't you see it?
Tell the truth
2.3.
B7
it? Can't you see it? Yeah. I can see it. I can see
to Coda
it. Yeah! I can see it, I can see it. Yeah.
Can't you see
C♯
4fr
G♯
4fr
B7
E
D.𝄋 al Coda
Tell the truth

CODA
B7
B7
__ it? Can't you see___ it?_ Yeah Wou,_ wou,__ wou,_ wou,
G
D
E
B
E
The whole world is shak - in' now. Can't you feel___ it?
B
E
B
E
G
D7
A new dawn is break - in' now, can't you see_
B7
__ it? Can't you see___ it?_ Yeah! I can see___ it, I can see_
__ it._ Yeah! I can see___ it. I can see___ it, Yeah! I can see_
__ it.__ I can see____ it, Yeah!
G
D
E

TOO BAD

WORDS & MUSIC BY ERIC CLAPTON.

A7
It's too bad I don't need you, because we get a-long so good.
E
B7
You must be think - ing 'bout this time,
A7
E
B7
E
that my poor heart is made of wood.
It's too bad
E7
A
E
I don't miss you, 'cause you are al-ways on my mind.
A7
It's too bad I don't miss you, 'cause you are al - ways on my
B7
mind.
I want to stay a - round, li'l' sil-ly girl,
A7
E
and learn to love you all the time.

53

THE SHAPE YOU'RE IN

A
E
A
tell by the smell that she'd had a few.
more wine than I've ev - er seen.
tell - in' you, ba - by, 'cause I've been there my-self.
E
C
A hold on, ba - by, don't you get too tight.
I sing, hold on, girl, don't get too tight.
I sing, hold on, girl, don't get too tight.
A
B
You start - ed ear - ly and we've got all night. You got - ta
E
C
A
take it ea - sy, take it slow. We don't want the whole
B
E
world to know a - bout the shape you're in.
G
A
A
B
Hey babe, the shape you're in, a - bout the

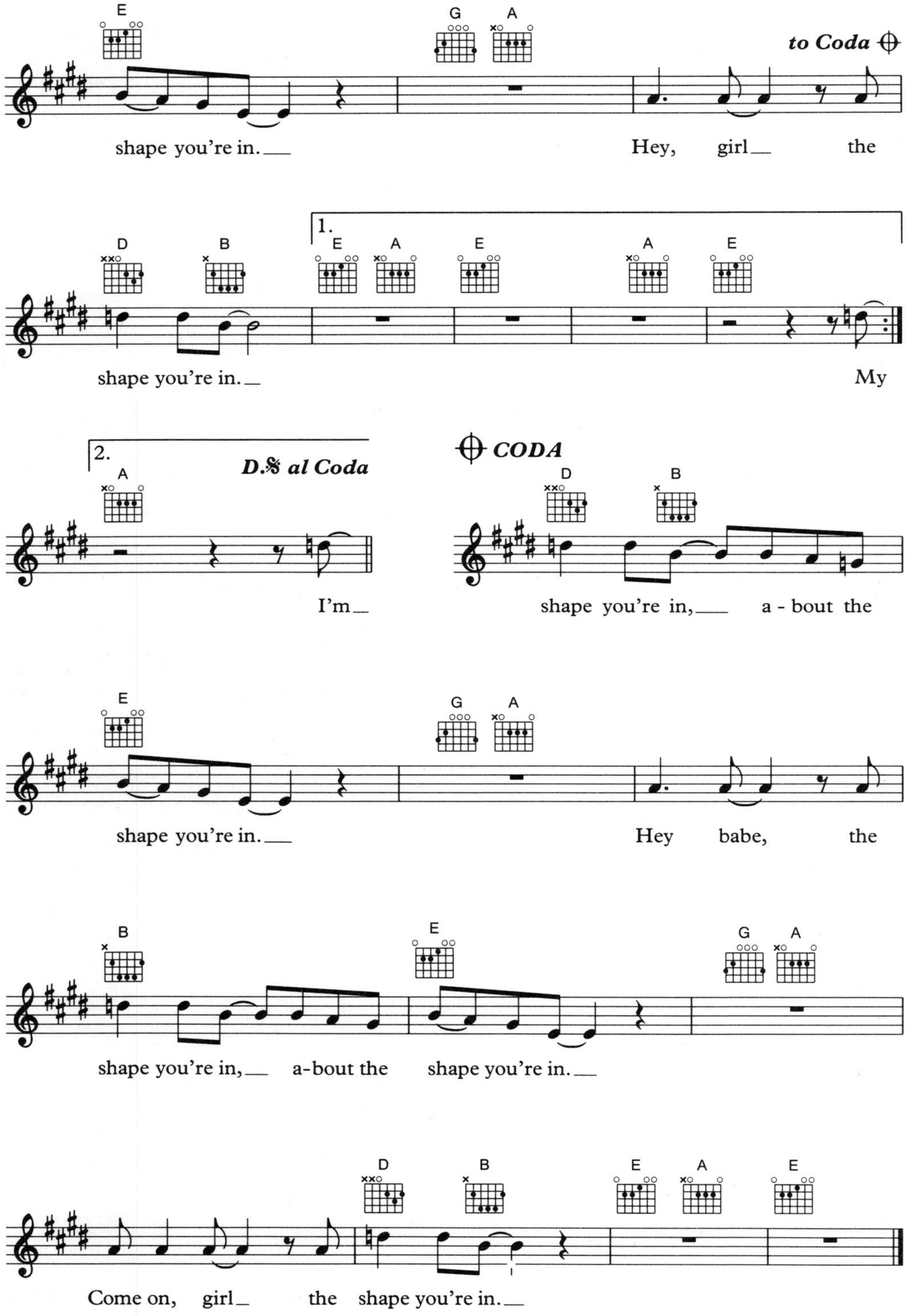
E
G
A
to Coda
shape you're in.
Hey, girl the
D
B
1.
E
A
E
A
E
shape you're in.
My
2.
A
D.S al Coda
CODA
D
B
I'm
shape you're in, a - bout the
E
G
A
shape you're in.
Hey babe, the
B
E
G
A
shape you're in, a-bout the shape you're in.
D
B
E
A
E
Come on, girl the shape you're in.

WATCH YOURSELF

WORDS & MUSIC BY BUDDY GUY.

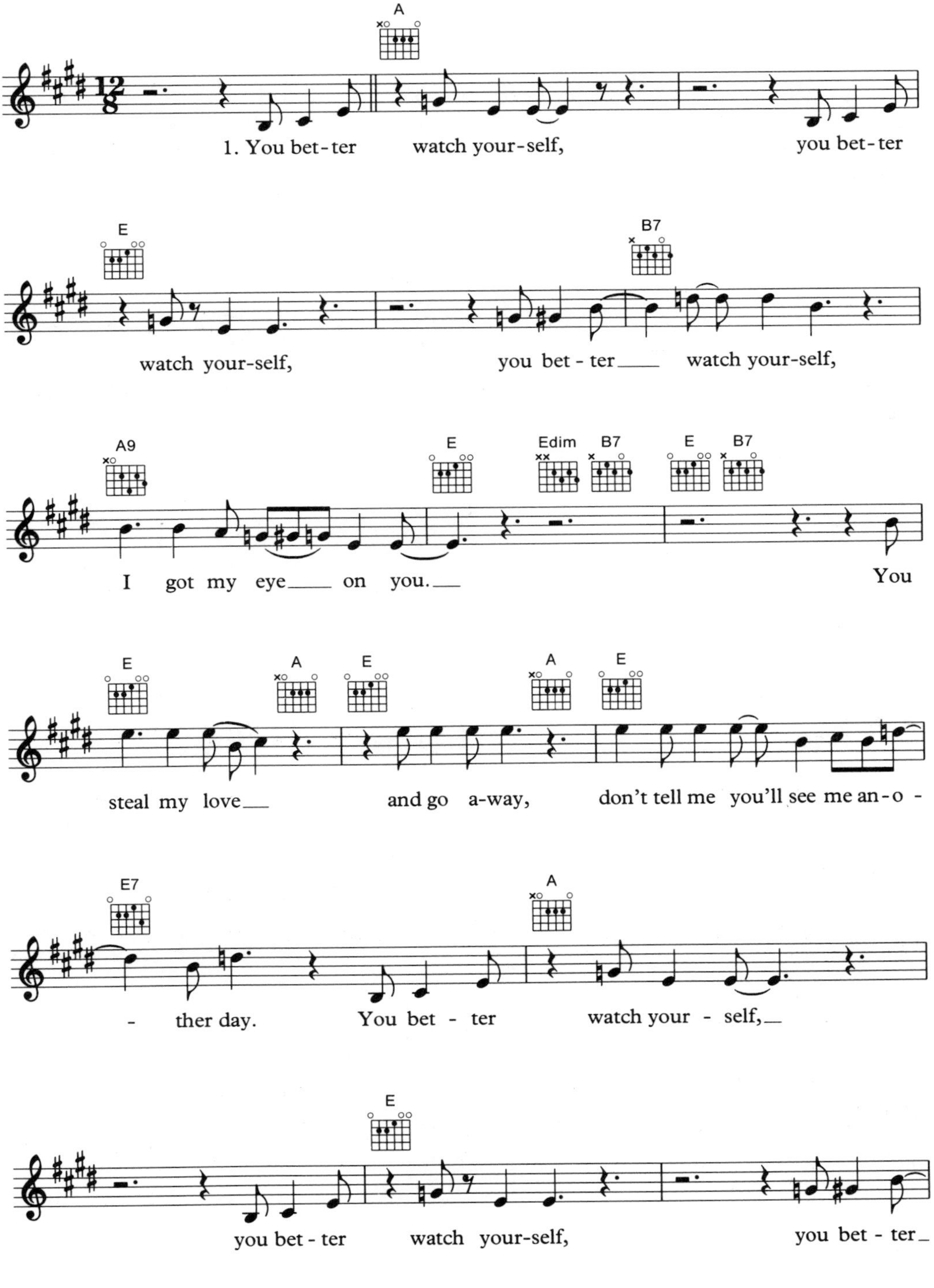

B7
A9
— watch your - self.
I got my eye — on you. —
E
Edim
B7
E
B7
E
A
— Yeah!
2. You gone and left — me, —
E
A
E
left me here to cry, —
y'know I — love — a - you know
E9
6fr
A
— you're my de - sire.
Watch your - self,
You bet - ter
E
E7
B7
watch your - self,
You bet - ter —
watch your - self, —
to Coda
1.2.
A9
E
Edim
B7
E
B7
I got my eye — on you. —
I — gave you
3.
E
B7
D.% al Coda
CODA
E
B7
You bet - ter

3. I gave you all my love
Everything too
A fine Cadillac
Tell me what you're gonna do
You better watch yourself . . .

4. People all talkin'
All over town
Sayin' you don't love me
And you're gonna put me down
You better watch yourself . . .

5. Tell me what's the matter
What you gonna do
You say you're gonna quit me
Then you say we're through
You better watch yourself . . .

WHITE ROOM

WORDS & MUSIC BY JACK BRUCE & PETE BROWN.

B♭ A C G
sun ne - ver shines; wait in this place where the
B♭ C D N.C.
sha - dows run from them - selves. You said
D C G/B B♭5 C5 3fr D C
no strings could se - cure you at the sta - tion.
G/B B♭5 C5 3fr D C G/B B♭5 C5 3fr
Plat - form tick - et, rest - less die - sels, good - bye
D C G/B B♭5 C5 3fr D C G/B B♭5 C5 3fr
win - dows. I walked in - to such a sad time at the
D C G/B B♭5 C5 3fr D C
sta - tion. As I walked out, felt my

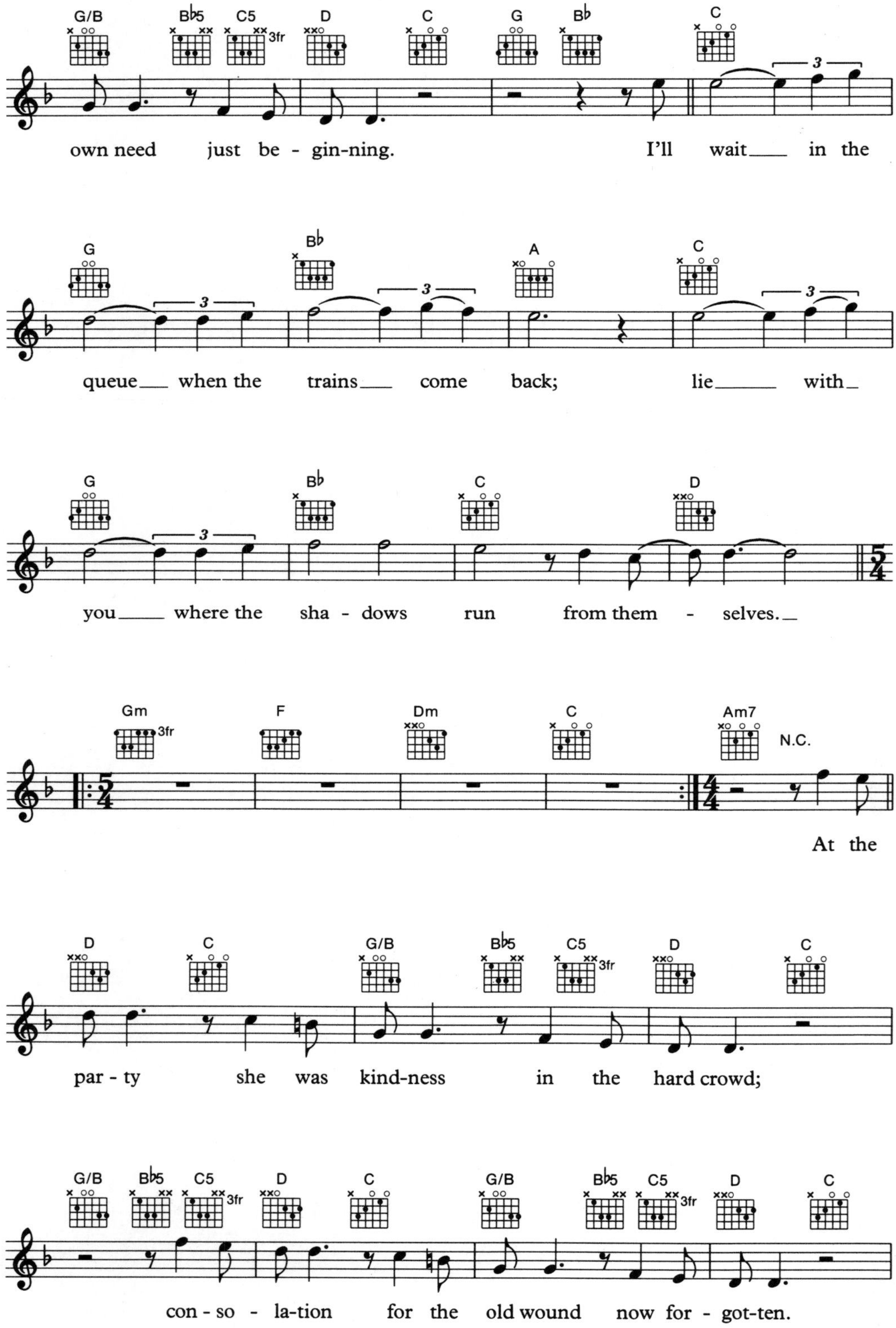
G/B Bb5 C5 3fr D C G Bb C
own need just be - gin-ning. I'll wait___ in the
G Bb A C
queue___ when the trains___ come back; lie___ with_
G Bb C D
you___ where the sha - dows run from them - selves._
Gm 3fr F Dm C Am7 N.C.
At the
D C G/B Bb5 C5 3fr D C
par - ty she was kind-ness in the hard crowd;
G/B Bb5 C5 3fr D C G/B Bb5 C5 3fr D C
con - so - la-tion for the old wound now for - got-ten.

G/B Bb5 C5 3fr D C G/B Bb C
Yel - low ti - gers crouched in jun-gles in the
D C G/B Bb5 D C
dark eyes.___ She's just dress-ing, good - bye
G/B Bb5 D C G/B Bb
win - dows_ tired___ star - lings. I'll
C G Bb A C
sleep__ in this place__ with the lone - ly crowd, lie___ in the
G Bb C D
dark___ where the sha - dows run from them - selves._
Gm 3fr F Dm C Am7 D C G/B Bb5 C5 3fr
Instrumental ad lib.

WHY DOES LOVE GOT TO BE SO SAD?

WORDS & MUSIC BY ERIC CLAPTON & BOBBY WHITLOCK.

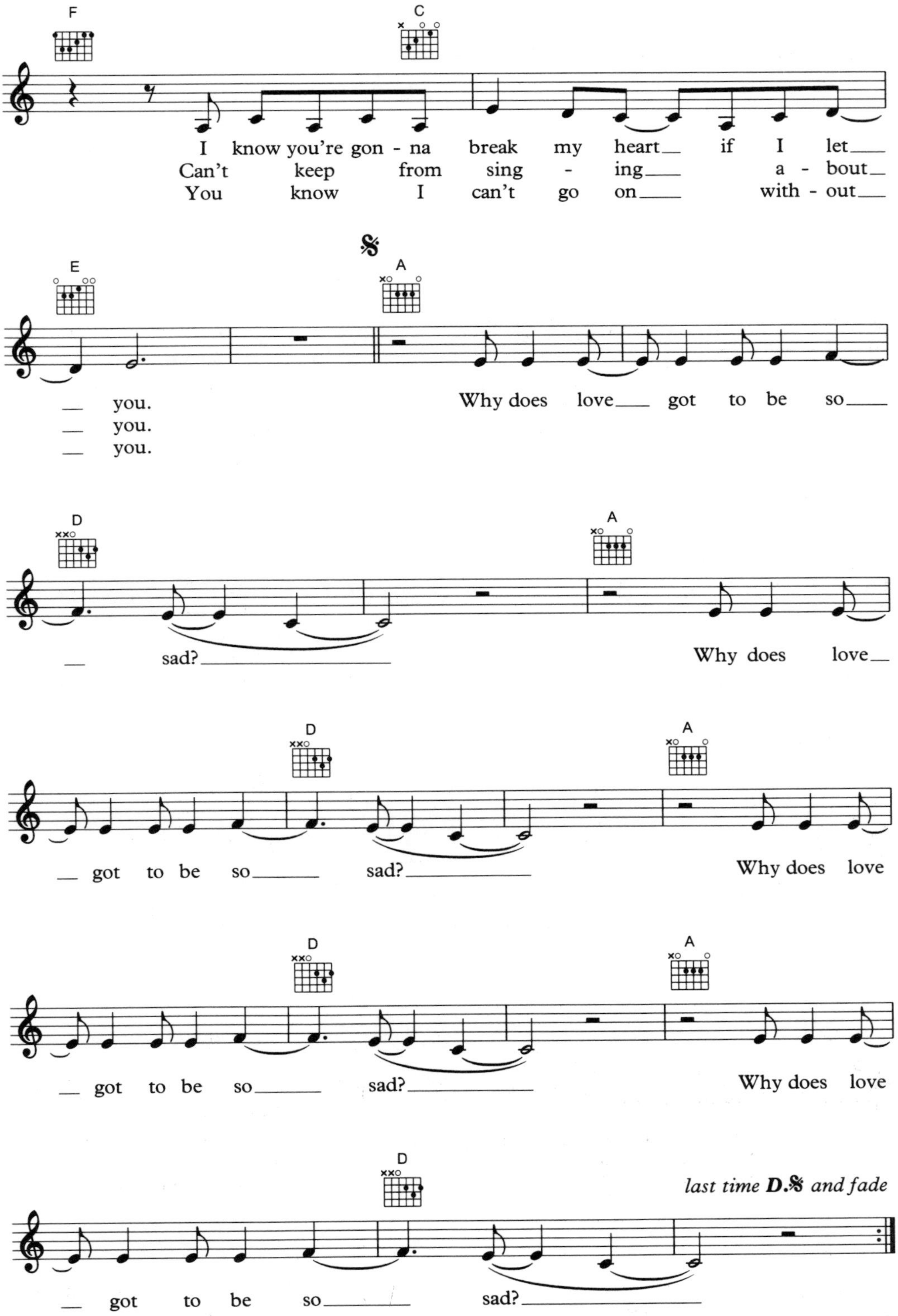
F
C
I know you're gon - na break my heart if I let
Can't keep from sing - ing a - bout
You know I can't go on with - out
E
A
you.
you.
you.
Why does love got to be so
D
A
sad?
Why does love
D
A
got to be so sad?
Why does love
D
A
got to be so sad?
Why does love
D
last time D.𝄋 and fade
got to be so sad?

57

WONDERFUL TONIGHT

WORDS & MUSIC BY ERIC CLAPTON.

1.
G
D/F♯
C
D
2.
D
I feel
C
D
G
D/F♯
won - der - ful be - cause I see the love light in your
Em
C
D
eyes. Then the won-der of it all is that you
C
D
G
just don't re - al - ize how much I love you.
D.C. al Coda
CODA
D/F♯
C
D
G
Em
Oh my
C
D
G
D/F♯
dar-ling, you are won-der - ful to-night.
C
D
C
D/F♯
C
D
G

WORRIED LIFE BLUES

WORDS & MUSIC BY MACEO MERRIWEATHER.

3. So many days, since you went away
I've had to worry, both night and day
But some day babe
I ain't gonna worry my life any more

4. So many nights, since you've been gone
I've been worried and leaving my life alone
But some day babe
I ain't gonna worry my life any more

5. So that's my story, and this is all I have to say to you
Goodbye babe, I don't care what you do
'Cause someday babe
Lord I ain't gonna worry my life any more

6. Oh! Lordy Lord, Oh! Lordy Lord
It hurt me so bad, for us to part
But some day babe
I ain't gonna worry my life any more